Southern Truths for Daily Living

Femininity is a plus in the business and social worlds.

❖

A woman can be both tough and nice.

❖

Temper progress with a healthy respect for tradition and history.

❖

Family and home take precedence over career.

❖

More flies are caught with honey than with vinegar.

❖

Men love strong, feminine women.

❖

Positive, optimistic attitudes are a necessity of life.

❖

Choose your battles carefully.

❖

Laugh at life's upsets and turn them to your advantage.

❖

Kindness and compassion are never out of date or out of style.

❖

Patience is a virtue and a necessity.

WHAT SOUTHERN WOMEN KNOW

(THAT EVERY WOMAN SHOULD)

Timeless Secrets to Get Everything You Want in Love, Life, and Work

RONDA RICH

A Perigee Book

A Perigee Book
Published by The Berkley Publishing Group
A division of Penguin Putnam Inc.
375 Hudson Street
New York, New York 10014

Book design by Lynn Amft

Published simultaneously in Canada.

G. P. Putnam's Son's edition: October 1999
First Perigee edition: September 2000

Perigee ISBN: 0-399-52627-7

The Penguin Putnam Inc. World Wide Web site address is
http://www.penguinputnam.com

The Library of Congress has catalogued the G. P. Putnam's Sons edition as follows:
Rich, Ronda.
What Southern women know (that every woman should) : timeless secrets to get everything you want in love, life, and work / Ronda Rich.
p. cm.
ISBN 0-399-14575-3
1. Women—Southern States—Psychology.
2. Women—Conduct of life. 3. Femininity. 4. Charm. I. Title
HQ1438.S63R5 1999 99-29355 CIP
305.4'0975—dc21

Printed in the United States of America

10 9 8 7 6 5 4

This book is dedicated to my mother, the executive producer of both the author and *many of the stories that lie within these pages, and to my agent, Richard Curtis, who saw what I did not see. My heartfelt gratitude to both.*

CONTENTS

What Southern Women Know

(THAT EVERY WOMAN SHOULD)

INTRODUCTION

Hail to the Belles: Strong as Oaks, Sweet as Honeysuckle

It is not unusual to find a strong, confident woman who thrives on progress and innovation. It *is* unusual, however, to find a strong, confident woman who tempers that toughness with a generous amount of grace and charm. Even more unusual is a woman with those traits who also clings to tradition, deeply treasures family, and cherishes history and heirlooms.

Unusual, that is, unless you're in the South, where these women are everywhere.

All my life, I have been surrounded by women whose carefully maintained exteriors beautifully camouflaged a fiery determination and indefatigable spirit. There are those who would call these women the heart of all things Southern. But they are much more than that—these women are the magnolia-scented breath which sustains the life of the South. They are the backbone of a region once laid waste by war, death, famine, and destruction; a region that resurrected itself through sheer willpower and an adamant refusal to accept defeat.

Much can be learned from these women because they know the misery of relentless adversity, the importance of progress that pays homage to proud tradition as well as the fine art of feminine toughness enchantingly embroidered with irresistible charm. The strong traditional Southern woman does not whine or complain. She conforms when necessary, but mostly she simply overcomes life's trials and tribulations.

From the bayous of Louisiana to the cotton fields of Mississippi to the mountains of North Georgia to the Carolina coast, these women have reigned supreme since April 12, 1861, when a single shot from Fort Sumter, South Carolina, changed their lives and charted a new course for all generations to come. The legacy, which began on that fateful day, has grown more bold, proud, and intense as the years have passed.

The humiliation of defeat gives birth to a resilience that bounces higher than any ups or downs in life. It teaches vital survival skills that, otherwise, would never be learned. Losing the Civil War is the best thing that ever happened to the women of the South. That loss taught them to be winners, a tradition that has been passed on as a flaming torch of pride to subsequent generations.

Defeat, famine, and destruction combined with the glorious prewar years of refinement and hospitality to create a unique breed—independent, indestructible women whose strong oak interiors are beautifully camouflaged with an overlay of sweet honeysuckle vines.

For the slave women freed by the war, the victory was, at best, hollow, because life became even more challenging. For the next century, they would fight to find their place in a culture to which they had once been captive. One hundred years of grappling and struggling has its rewards, too, and those women bequeathed their hard-earned strength, dignity, and indestructible spirit to their heirs. From their loins would spring the grandchildren who would rise up as civil rights activists. Although discrimination had long held the entire world in its ugly grasp, it was from the heart of the South that the civil rights movement reared its indignant head. It was powered, quite simply, by Southern mothers who taught their sons to be proud and to fight for a gentler, more loving nation; mothers who believed that adversity of any kind could be overcome through hard work and dedication. Then, of course, there were the women who fought in the trenches beside them during the movement and used every ounce of their Southern womanhood to fight the war of an entire nation.

Whether we are descendants of plantation owners, farmers, slaves, moonshiners, tenant farmers, craftsmen, riverboat captains, or merchants, we are the daughters of the South, the embodiment of moxie, determination, and tender femininity. Molded by history, wedded to tradition, committed to the future, we tackle life with a customized and paradoxical blend of toughness and kindness.

Common threads of charm, strength, and resilience are woven carefully through the South's cultural fabric, weaving together women from different races and economic levels. Be they Appalachian women, often strangers to common luxuries, or freed slaves whose great-granddaughters became civil rights activists, or the millions of middle-class women who successfully bridge the gaps among home, family, and career, Southern women brazenly attack the storms of life. With unique style, they wear the battle armor of soldiers while maintaining the soft, virginal hearts of ingenues. Southern women staunchly believe that it *is* possible to be both tough warriors *and* sensuous, delicate lovers.

I am both inspired and amused by the images of the strong women whom I have loved as family and admired as my friends. My grandmother, who fought the sad poverty of the Appalachian Mountains to raise a family of nine, scrubbed laundry on a washboard in a nearby stream until the blood of her raw hands stained the clothing. This family of a circuit-riding preacher was so poor that the Depression that later seized the nation in a merciless grip went completely unnoticed by them. It was not possible to be poorer than they already were.

As the daughter of a prosperous merchant and landowner, my grandmother had willingly traded a comfortable life for one of uncertainty, and she did so in the name of great love. In the tradition of other strong Southern women, she never complained, never regretted the choice she had made. Love and family, she always believed, were more important than material possessions. She chose instead to count her blessings and at the age of eighty-nine died with the memories of a happy, love-filled life.

My own mother learned well at her mother's knee and proved to be another splendid example of silk blended with steel. When I was a preschooler and the actions of a dishonest employee threatened to destroy my father's business and push him into bankruptcy, it was my mother's strength and insurmountable energy that held our family together.

The employee, using my father's name, amassed a huge

debt with one of Dad's business's suppliers and then skipped town. Daddy owned an automotive repair business and the employee, no more than a runner who picked up parts at supply stores and made deliveries, used his position to charge many thousands of dollars worth of merchandise to daddy's in-store accounts. He left my dad owing more money than he could make in two years. With an uncompromising sense of integrity, my daddy refused to file for bankruptcy and promised the supplier that somehow, in some way, the debt would be completely repaid.

Mama, shielded from the workplace by three decades of marriage, immediately rose to the occasion. She had no formal education or training but was a talented dressmaker. For three years, she labored uncomplainingly in a hot, labor-intensive sewing plant, happy for the money that paid the mortgage and other bills and enabled Daddy to pay off the ill-begotten debt.

A magnolia blossom never falls far from the tree and, as a result, I never cease to be amused by an image conjured up of my sister on a muggy, late-summer afternoon as she chased stray cows. Cattle, which escape from a pasture through ingenious means, are a horror to their owners because they can cause serious car accidents or disappear forever. In other words, when the cows are out, it's an emergency.

That day when the SOS filtered through the family that several cows had escaped from Daddy's pasture, one by one we converged at my parents' home from our various jobs and schools to help round up the wayward livestock. My sister, upon receiving the call, had thrown down the telephone and dashed out of her office, calling over her shoulder to her employees that she was leaving as she darted out the back door.

I will carry in my mind forever the image of my exquisitely coifed sister in an expensive bright yellow designer suit chasing cattle through briar patches and waist-high grass, stopping only momentarily by the creek before pulling her skirt above her knees and wading across. It should be properly noted here that Southern women always have a pair of flats available for such emergencies when our usual, beloved high heels just won't do.

Of course, sibling rivalry runs strong and sometimes irresponsibly rampant in my family. So not to be outdone, I one-upped her later by corralling a stray bull that had brought traffic to a dead stop. While other drivers pondered what to do, I figuratively grabbed the bull by the horns and literally herded the stubborn animal back into captivity.

"That's the most amazing thing I ever saw," a man commented when the task was completed.

I shrugged nonchalantly as I got back into my car. To me, it was not a big deal, because Southern women are courageous, undaunted by challenges, and are quick to roll up our sleeves to get the job done. We believe that with a little elbow grease and a lot of perseverance, *anything* is possible. That's why a hundred and fifteen pounds of me was able to prevail over fifteen hundred pounds of beast.

Women of the South are proud, hardworking, and dedicated to personal improvement. We want to be our best and look our best. It is not acceptable to sacrifice one for the other. My niece, Nicole, crowned a beauty queen many times, is a prime example. She graduated at the top of her high school, college, and graduate-school classes. Every day, Nicole works herself into an unglamorous sweat and disheveled appearance as a loving, compassionate physical therapist for geriatric patients. She listens patiently to their rambling, endless stories and asks the right questions at the appropriate time. Compassion for the elderly and tolerance of their eccentricities is another Southern trait. Nicole will pat cousin Wilma's aging hand and assure her that Burt will soon arrive at the nursing home for his daily visit.

Wilma, well into her eighties, is a cousin on my daddy's side. For thirty years, she has believed that she is married to Burt Reynolds.

"Burt can't make it to my birthday party," she said sweetly one afternoon, with a sigh. "He's in Hollywood making a movie, but our son is coming."

We indulge the spinster's fantasy because in the South, people like Wilma aren't called "crazy" but, rather, are praised for being "eccentric." We delight in and extol the virtues of these eccentrics because they add flavor to our culture and color to our celebrated stories.

Then, of course, there was my grandmother, also on Daddy's side, who would entertain guests daintily sipping tea with the cold, dark steel of a Smith & Wesson nuzzled in her vast lap.

"They were here again last night," she would remark in between sips, delicately touching the corners of her mouth with a napkin.

"Who?"

"Those men who are always walkin' on top of the roof. The same ones who are tryin' to drive me crazy."

We would nod politely. No one would dare to dispute a two-hundred-pound woman with a loaded pistol. Then she would beam a radiant smile filled with self-satisfaction.

"I think I got one of 'em last night. I heard him screamin' when I shot through the ceiling." She pointed to a new hole.

"See that hole over yonder? That's where I got the low-down varmint."

It is probably more than a mite suspicious that both of these eccentrics spring from Daddy's side of the family. But that's just about as far into that closet of family skeletons as I wish to go. I still have to live with these people, you know.

Nicole, a normally prissy blonde who shows up for church on Sunday beautifully turned out in frock and hat but isn't afraid of sweat and toil, isn't an exception—she is merely an example of the many women like her throughout the South.

One of the greatest inspirations in my life has been a woman named Katherine, who raised five rambunctious children by herself after a divorce. She worked at three jobs to make ends meet, attended every school function, and never missed a church meeting. Her youngest son, Andrew, was a sensational athlete and at the age of fifteen, colleges were already courting the quiet, modest young man for their football programs. During a routine preseason physical, the doctor discovered that Andrew was in an advanced stage of cancer. The announcement sent waves of shock and sadness spiraling through Andrew's family, friends and coaches. Since the quiet young man had never complained of pain or discomfort, the diagnosis was completely unexpected. Later, as we watched him suffer medical treatments and the resulting torments with somber dignity, we realized that complaining was simply not his style.

With no preamble and very little warning, Andrew's left leg was amputated above the knee. The doctors said he would never play football again, but Andrew said he would. The youngster possessed the same spunky spirit as his mother and, inspired by the example she had set, several months later he proved true to his word.

One cold, frosty fall night, a stadium crowd watched as Andrew hopped out onto the field to take his place on the defensive line. The crowd held its collective breath as the ball was snapped, the lines collided, and one by one the players dropped, all except Andrew who threw his full strength into fighting his opponent until he had knocked him to the ground. When Andrew succumbed to the horrible disease a few months later, the lovely Katherine faced his death bravely and celebrated his life rather than mourning his death. She never said, "Woe is me," only "I was so blessed to have had him as a son."

A lesson I learned long ago came from a tiny, ninety-pound woman of the mountains who had watched as her husband and children died one by one and left her alone to suffer life's indignities. Although her hands were badly gnarled from arthritis and callused from years of hard physical labor, she still managed to plant and harvest vegetables and chop firewood for her wood stove.

At the age of ninety-two, her life was ebbing slowly to an end as she reflected on the blessings and misfortunes of her long life: "It ain't been easy," she said softly. "But God never puts more on ya than ya can bear." A twinkle of hard-learned wisdom flickered across her pale blue eyes washed lighter by the passage of time. She shook her head and sighed. "But He shore kin bend 'cha double sometimes!"

These are the women of the South—proud, strong, gentle, undaunted by hard work or hard times. The ability to survive comes as naturally to us as the honeysuckle vines that grow wild and fragrantly scent the air on a warm summer's evening. Yet, such resilient strength and emotional toughness is not brought to bear at the sacrifice of feminine softness. We have found a way to combine the best of all worlds—traditional femininity and endearing charm with worldly shrewdness and cunning ability.

While hard-won survival often requires a masculine-like strength, Southern women deceptively decorate their power with charm, good manners, and a bright, cheery attitude. Unequivocally, the most important bit of wisdom possessed by Southern women is that the syrupy stickiness of sweet honey always catches more flies than the bitterness of liquid vinegar.

The titillating secrets of Southern women are many, most guarded as cautiously as their family recipes and heirlooms. We are a culture known for our kindness and generosity, but that largesse has never extended to sharing the secrets of our Southern feminine souls.

Until now.

In a world often conflicted with disagreements, anger, and greed, it is time to practice captivating charm and impeccable manners again. In a universe of people with too many obligations and too little time, there is room for increased thoughtfulness and kindness.

It is, quite simply, time to apply a soothing salve of Southern comfort to the world. It is, after all, what Southern women know best and, many believe, that *every* woman should know as well.

CHAPTER ONE

It's More Than the Drawl, Y'all

WHAT IS IT about Southern women that is so devastatingly irresistible? What is the magnetic force that pulls both men and women to them as easily as a pine tree grows on a north Georgia mountain?

The allure of Southern women is undeniable. Many men are captivated by these charming examples of luscious womanhood. Other women are mystified when it comes to trying to decipher and imitate the indescribable Southern appeal that is capable of melting the hardest of hearts. Even the South's most treacherous enemy, General William Tecumseh Sherman, fell victim in his youth to the fluttery charms of a Georgia belle, the sister of one of his West Point classmates. It was a deep, heartfelt affection he carried throughout his life.

What do Southern women have that other women do not possess?

It's more than the drawl, y'all.

Our nemeses believe that our entire charm lies within the cadence of our enticing drawl. Not true. Admittedly it *is* an attention getter outside the South; however, without substance behind those lyrical words, the façade would quickly crumble. The drawl—which accents the rhapsodic blend of beauty, grace, charm, ingenuity, and strength—is nothing more than the gorgeous red bow that completes the package.

The truth is that our secrets lie in a combination of many skills and talents, supported by years of training and generations of tradition. Can it be copied and emulated by non-Southern women? Absolutely! Is it easy? About as easy as Aunt Ozelle's homemade chicken and dumplings, and that was only easy after a little studying and a lot of practicing. But, in the end, the results, like the chicken and dumplings, are sensational and well worth the effort. Success, after all, *seldom* comes easily and is rarely accomplished on the first try.

So what is it about Southern women that is as intoxicating to men as a sniff of homemade peach brandy? What is it that allows them to blossom as beautifully as the dogwood trees that dot Atlanta's Peachtree Street? Or to adapt as well to the business world as the best oil man in Texas?

Simply put, Southern women have the ability to survive in a man's world while wrapped in a pouf of flowery femininity and gracious, thoughtful manners. Southern women often overemphasize femininity and use it as one of their most successful tools professionally and socially. While other women often think that the best way to compete in a man's world is to hide any traces of femininity or to imitate a man as closely as possible, Southern women are appalled by such thoughts! We treasure our womanliness and celebrate it. In fact, we shamelessly flaunt it.

Men soak this up the way a hot, dusty cotton field absorbs rain on a summer's day. They *love* feminine women in both the social world and the business world.

Thirty or forty years ago when women were entering the business world en masse, it was necessary to suppress a large amount of femininity in order to be taken seriously. Fortunately, the trails have now been blazed to the point that women travel the same superhighways as their male colleagues. Gender equality does not mean that gender has to be interchangeable in all ways, except physical. Southern women know we can have professional and personal equality without sacrificing our femininity, good manners, tender compassion, principles, or humor.

Therein lies the key to our success.

We love being soft, feminine women on the outside with an interior that is as formidable as the coal mines of Kentucky. We are an enchanting blend of silk and steel, a contradictory mixture of demure sensuality and robust independence, of exuberant spirit and subtle class.

When a woman rejects her feminine side, she disposes of her most effective shield for battle in the business world. It's like going out in the rain without an umbrella. Umbrellas can seem boring in their utilitarian practicality. For example, have you ever been the unenthusiastic recipient of an umbrella as a gift?

"Surely," you think to yourself, "she could have thought of a better gift than *this*."

But then it rains and you can think of no gift you would rather possess than the once unappreciated umbrella. Our femininity is like that umbrella. It is a wonderful gift that is often underappreciated, but there is, in fact, no greater protection against the storms of life.

Men have an innate instinct to treat women with courtesy and respect, even at times to protect them. Because of this instinct, professional men would never think of harming, undercutting, or back-stabbing a traditionally feminine woman. It goes against their primal instincts.

However, if a woman behaves in a masculine manner and fights by a man's rules, she stupidly tosses this wonderful shield of protection aside. Men react to these women by throwing traditional custom and behavior to the wind. They fight even more aggressively against these hard-edged women than they do against other men. In fact, they often will not hesitate to professionally annihilate a manlike woman.

They'll attack because men hate to see a poor imitation of themselves. They also don't like being around women who make them feel uncomfortable by behaving in a nontraditional manner. Neither do other women. That's why tough, bitchy women never rise to the greatest heights of corporate success. They disturb the synergy in a company, and that, in turn, makes them ineffective and unpromotable. They also alienate people as they try to climb the ladder of success, which is why they get caught on a rung somewhere in the middle.

Take a look around you and you'll see that the supersuccessful professional women are those who were smart enough to combine the best of all worlds. They are gracious, smart women who put employees and colleagues at ease as charming hostesses do, yet they have the ability to motivate and to generate success. And, most important, they do not sacrifice their all-too-important feminine qualities. They accentuate their natural gifts rather than eliminate them.

Southern women cleverly realize that femininity is extremely useful in professional situations. Of course, we probably *do* use it more than other women throughout the world, but it *does* work. So, why quibble about using your God-given gifts? Just go ahead and do it. Then, sit back, sip a mint julep and enjoy the fruits of your labor.

The biggest key to a Southern woman's success in life is charm. It's that simple. Southern women are as charming at the office as they are in their homes where they amply dispense that precious commodity known as Southern hospitality.

Charm is the art of making others feel good about themselves *and* about you. Femininity and oozing charm are a Southern woman's trademarks. We're specifically trained from the cradle to be feminine, but our charm is painstakingly developed. We spend years learning to wink, smile, flutter, flatter, and bedazzle.

And, honey, does it work!

But being the perfect Southern woman doesn't just happen. My friend Virgie, a wise, worldly Mississippi belle, purrs seductively, "Darlin', I have made a *study* of how to be the perfect Southern woman. Anyone who thinks all of this comes easy, just doesn't *realize* the work involved. But Southern women do not mind work; that's why we're so successful."

That's why I know that anyone who applies a little effort can emulate the fine art of Southern womanhood. The South does have its share of failures—those distasteful women who bring shame to the dignity of our proud honor. Lazy, that's what we call them. They are the women who spend their days popping bonbons, staring mindlessly at soap operas, and bringing no value to society through professional or volunteer participation. And—horror of horrors—wearing not even one stitch of makeup even though they'll only be seen that day by the family cat, not to mention one dissatisfied husband. We're talking not even a tint of pink on their colorless lips!

Shocking, yes, but a measly few of these women *do* reside within the hallowed confines of the South. Thankfully, though, these failures are few and far between.

We don't, however, hesitate to criticize that rare Southern woman who breaks the sacred rule of devotion to femininity, beauty, and charm. When she ceases to care how she looks, we cease to care about her. Brutality, thy name is Southern woman! We ignore them, scorn them, mock them, and hope, in general, that they will just go away and stop embarrassing us.

But, enough of those betrayers of a proud heritage; let's talk about the majority of Southern women who receive the doting affection and attention of all those around them. The women who epitomize the breed that Hollywood loves, Broadway adores, and the world admires. The kind of woman that Fitzgerald married and Faulkner loved. The kind of woman also capable, in her own right, of writing a book and winning the coveted Pulitzer as no fewer than ten Southern women—Julia M. Peterkin, Margaret Mitchell, Marjorie Kinnan Rawlings, Ellen Glasgow, Harper Lee, Shirley Ann Grau, Katherine Anne Porter, Eudora Welty, Alice Walker, and Anne Tyler—have done.

Two of these women—Ms. Mitchell and Ms. Lee—created twentieth-century masterpieces, virtually unequaled in the dynamic combination of critical acclaim and commercial success garnered by their respective works, *Gone with the Wind* and *To Kill a Mockingbird.* Many readers have considered it sadly disappointing—in fact, downright tragic—that each of these authors from the Deep South wrote one, lone work of magnificent literature. There were no prequels, no sequels, not even as much as a five-hundred-word essay.

But the Georgia-born Mitchell and the Alabama-born Lee were obvious products of Southern genteel upbringing, the offspring of mothers who probably preached that familiar sermon of many Southern mothers, "Always make a graceful exit while you're still the toast of the party. Don't ever outstay your welcome."

Southern women are not quitters. Sometimes, though, we know when we've done our best work and it's time to stop. It's then that we whisper our thank-yous, say our good-byes, and slip out of the party while we're still the star. We don't ever try to outdo ourselves when we know that it simply cannot be done.

The enticing sparkle that shimmers on the surface is like the icing on a well-designed confectionery concoction. The foundation of this beguiling charm that has held men captivated for centuries is unbreakable self-confidence.

Most Southern women are extraordinarily self-confident. This results from a security provided by survival know-how and because Southern women take a great deal of pride in their appearance. A strong, secure Southern woman unhesitatingly compliments another woman both to her face *and* behind her back. She sincerely praises another woman's beauty, talents, and clothes. She isn't jealous. If she admires something that someone else has, she sets her mind to getting one for herself rather than envying the other woman. This creates a special bond among Southern women and enables us to share our strengths with one another.

Southern mystique is a paradoxical blend of many attributes and attitudes, which is why no one before has ever been able to clone a version of that delectable, demure, and devastatingly cunning creature.

But now you can.

Wouldn't you love to wrap men around your little finger or to create a paradise of sublime contentment at work? Here's how to start:

Create warmth wherever you go. Be warm and inviting in relationships, with family, at the office, in your home, in the rooms you enter. Be open and enticing rather than cool and aloof. Shower those in your presence with engaging smiles. Make everyone feel welcomed into your world. Southern hospitality is the standard by which the rest of the world is judged. That special brand of hospitality begins with tremendous warmth, openness, and the giving of one's self.

Always notice everyone around you. As you walk through the mall, down the aisle at church, or along the hallway at the office, acknowledge everyone with a nod, a smile, and a word. Don't allow yourself to be caught up in your own world, oblivious of other people—even if they are strangers. This kind of openness is a very important part of charm. People mirror your treatment of them. If you are warm, you receive warmth in return. Coolness is reciprocated with aloofness. People respond eagerly to warmth, which enables you to get more of what you want from life because people are more willing to help you.

Establish instant rapport. When introduced to someone, lean toward the person (out of your personal space and into theirs) to establish immediate intimacy. Stop a foot or so from the other person's face, smile, establish eye contact, and say a few kind words. In the South, we hate instant potatoes, but we love instant warmth!

Treat everyone with equal kindness and respect. From cabdrivers to waitresses to your boss to your prospective mother-in-law. Shower them all with smiles and courtesy. Everyone, regardless of his or her position in life, deserves courtesy, respect, and kind words. Daddy always said, "There are no big 'I's' and little 'you's.' We're all the same in God's eyes." Besides, such regular use of your charm and warmth will make you even more irresistible. Remember: Practice makes perfect, so practice on everyone.

Be gracious, thoughtful, and always considerate of others and their feelings. It is possible to be both tough and nice. You do not have to sacrifice one for the other; you must only know when to use each one. However, 98 percent of the time, nice works best.

More flies are caught with honey than with vinegar. Charm, sweetness, and friendly, thoughtful consideration are a woman's best allies for getting what she wants in life.

Think positive thoughts. Doing so will clearly radiate in your face, which will create enhanced beauty as well as increase your charm. Others are undeniably drawn to happy, positive people.

Be utterly feminine. Men cannot resist a feminine woman—personally or professionally. In business, men become mentors to these women, enhancing their careers and professional knowledge. Personally, they become protectors, never suspecting that the woman is the true backbone of the relationship. In the South, our secret motto is "Let him think he's the boss, but we know who the boss really is!" Men love strong, but soft, feminine women. They are enthralled by them. They are not personally or professionally attracted to women who conduct themselves like men—especially for long-term relationships.

Flaunt your femininity. From bedrooms to boardrooms, femininity will be your greatest asset and ally. Don't hide it or be ashamed of it. Southern mothers raise their daughters to "be a lady in the drawing room, a tigress in the bedroom." We use our femininity to seduce both sexually and socially.

In the business and social worlds, femininity is a plus, not a minus. Boldly use your femininity professionally and personally. We socially flirt (see chapter 7) at the office, wear feminine, soft clothing, and shamelessly use our feminine wiles to get what we want professionally—plum assignments, transfers, raises, and promotions. We never cross the line into inappropriateness, but we have been known to stretch it to the limits.

Femininity requires attention to detail. A significant amount of femininity happens naturally. But perfect femininity combines unconscious natural ability with conscious effort and diligent work. It's the package of options added to the standard equipment. It's the delicious difference between a cake made from a store-bought mix and one made from scratch.

Those special details include lingerie that is color coordinated to the outfit you're wearing, toenail polish that is coordinated to fingernail polish that is coordinated to lip gloss. It may sound like an awful lot of work, but it's worth the effort.

Even if the rest of the world doesn't know you're wearing sexy, red lingerie under that red suit, *you* know it. And because you know it, you feel sexy and act sexy. It's one of the small finishing touches that give you an indefinable edge over the competition. How many times have you seen a seemingly unremarkable woman who had men falling at her feet and wondered what was going on? Chances are she was wearing a red lace demi-bra with matching thong. She felt sexy, and men were naturally responding to the sexiness oozing from every pore of her body.

Another trick of the Southern trade: We powder and perfume not only ourselves *but* our bedsheets.

Say "no" nicely. Okay, heightened sensuality is going to bring attention from men—both wanted and unwanted attention. Southern women know how to say "no" nicely but firmly. We don't slap, yell, cry "sexual harassment," sue, or berate a man with a string of profanities. Instead, we sweetly remove his hands and say with an enchanting, lilting tone, "Now, be nice!" Or if he's married, "My, my, my! Somehow, I just don't think your wife would be amused by this one little bit!" Those words are punctuated with a warning look, the seriousness of which is masked with a smile.

When a man suggests an intimate situation or a close male friend suddenly professes feelings for us, we laugh delightedly and say, "You are so silly! Will you please be serious!" Then we quickly change the subject to something more appropriate. His feelings are never hurt and since he isn't belittled, he does not become an enemy. He becomes a friend who gains new respect for such a classy woman.

I defy anyone to tell me that this approach does not work. I have spent my professional life in male-dominated worlds from sports reporting to motor-sports marketing to the corporate world. Never once in hundreds of attempts has this tactic failed me. In fact, a few men, who later became friends, admitted, "I've never been turned down so nicely and sweetly. You didn't bruise my ego at all or make me feel like a jerk."

Southern women are charmers in all situations—even unpleasant ones. We always remember to treat everyone with respect and graciousness.

High heels are always in vogue. They give an alluring line to the leg and put that undeniable prissiness in your walk. Of course, we Southern women exaggerate that wiggle—especially when the occasion calls for it.

Don't hesitate to compliment—especially other women. Praise another woman's beauty, talents, and clothes. We are inspired by another's beauty—not jealous. Being encouraged by the beauty and talents of others pushes us toward constant self-improvement. Complimenting others creates warmth and shows a self-confidence that is always attractive to others.

Deliver panache, your own special style. Be adventurous in finding your unique look and don't settle for one specific one. Bounce from designer suits to trendy apparel to a mixture of both. Recently, I garnered many compliments on a "thrown together" outfit that consisted of a pricey top from Nieman Marcus, an inexpensive skirt from Kmart, strappy pumps from JCPenney, and the perfect hat from Bloomingdale's. It's how you carry yourself that defines your look.

Do not be a shrinking violet who blends in with drab gray wallpaper. Wear lots of bright colors—they make you stand out in a crowd. Southern women try to outdo one another at social events. As she walks down the aisle, a Southern bride is nearly blinded by all the bright dresses and pampered beauties in the audience.

Sassy self-confidence requires faith in yourself and your ability to achieve. Remember: Faith is like a muscle; the more you exercise it, the stronger it becomes. Use that strong faith to chase away the insidious doubts that threaten success and self-confidence. Do not forget that it is within your power to succeed or to fail. Southern women are fiercely proud and therefore staunchly geared toward success in all they do.

Be spunky, not aggressive; assertive, not brash. Southern women are not timid in going after what we want, but we do it in a charming, self-assured manner, not in a rude, win-at-all-costs mode. When we get what we want, we don't step over the scattered bodies as we make our victorious exit. We walk out with heads held high, knowing that everyone was treated ethically and respectfully.

Karen is one of my dearest friends in the world and the only roommate I've ever had. After I shared space with such a captivating, entertaining Southern belle, all other possible roommates paled in comparison.

She deliciously blends charm and spunk in such a delightful way that she can boldly ask someone the most incredible question and charm him into giving her the most honest, forthright answer possible.

Karen, as one of the top female vocalists in Southern gospel music, has used her compelling charm to win award after award and fan after fan. As is typical of most Southern women, her bubbly, affable personality beautifully covers a steely determination and gutsy approach to life. Where giants might tremble, she boldly marches in and tranquilizes with charm. That's why it isn't unusual at all that Karen should decide to take it upon herself to solve a mystery that has intrigued the world for quite a while.

One night while on tour, she found herself performing with the legendary J. D. Sumner and the Stamps. The Stamps traveled extensively with Elvis Presley, who was passionate in both his love of Southern gospel music *and* his worship of the rich baritone voice of his devoted friend J. D. Sumner.

After the concert ended, Karen boldly marched over to the Stamps' bus and broke her own long-standing rule of protocol by knocking on the bus of a fellow entertainer. J. D. opened the door and welcomed her warmly.

"Hello, honey, come right on up here," he greeted Karen.

Karen climbed on the bus and, with no preamble, she launched into her mission with patented charm. "J. D., I need to ask you something because I want to hear it right from the horse's mouth."

The famed baritone leaned forward and rested his elbows on his knees, interested in hearing the question. "What is it, sweetheart? Ask me anything."

"Is Elvis *really* dead?" she blurted out.

"As dead as a doornail," he replied in that deep, throaty voice that had serenaded the throng of people at Elvis's funeral. "I saw him, I touched him, and I know it. He's dead, all right. Any more questions?"

"No, that's it. That's what I wanted to know. Thank you."

And, then with the same swiftness with which she had entered, she exited the bus. J. D. Sumner, famous for his gruff protection of his dear friend's privacy and dignity, might have been insulted by the temerity of someone else asking such a question. But when an enchanting Southern lady asked in a spunky, rather than irreverent, brash manner, he was not offended.

He was charmed.

CHAPTER TV

Charm That Disarms

So much has been written about the charms of Southern women that it certainly warrants a chapter of its own. The charm of all Southerners—women and men—intrigues a world that yearns to unlock the secret and use it, too.

"What is it about you guys that is so charming?" a woman in Los Angeles asked me as her eyes carefully searched my face. "I can't quite put my finger on it, but you Southerners certainly have more than your share."

"Oh, yes. I have heard stories of you Southerners and your Southern hospitality," a proper Briton with a clipped, aristocratic accent commented to me during a trip to London. "What do you do that is so bloody spectacular?"

Southern women are artists who carefully package all the necessary elements into a portrait worthy of Van Gogh's signature. We drape ourselves in beautiful, bright colors, flirt shamelessly, and, above all, are always kind and thoughtful to others. This trademark of graciousness and consideration of others is an appealingly seductive lure.

That is one of our biggest assets.

It is what draws people to us as magically and as forcefully as the Mississippi River pulls other waters into its strong

t. People like to be treated with kindness and thought-ness. It feels good. Really good. And when they are treated that way, they respond in similar fashion. In short, folks mimic our treatment of them.

Today's world is so busy and hectic that people often think mostly of themselves and their families. No one sets out to be intentionally rude or inconsiderate; it's just that there's so much on people's minds, they don't stop to think. We Southerners, on the other hand, are frequently thinking of others—not because we're superhumans or extraordinarily special, but because we are *trained* to think of others. It's our way of life.

It is a practice instilled in us from childhood and one that enables us to think of the little things—the things that mean so much to others. It is not uncommon for Southern women to carefully weigh any decision—large or small—against how that decision will touch those on the outer edges of their lives.

"I need to have knee surgery, but I am going to wait until my daughter-in-law has her baby and has fully recovered because I want to be in condition to help her all I can," a Southern woman might comment.

Another might explain, "I found the most darling dress that I wanted to buy for my parents' golden anniversary party. But the dress is bright green and mother *hates* that color on me. Since it's her party, I'm not about to wear something she doesn't like. It wouldn't be very considerate."

"I was going to have Charlie's birthday party at that wonderful new restaurant in midtown, but the owner was exceedingly rude to my best friend the other day, so I absolutely refuse to spend any money with him."

These are true examples of women of the South who are conscious of how their actions might have an impact on others. If you're not used to thinking that way, you have to train yourself. But it can be done. To be quite honest, I sometimes have to refocus and fine-tune my thought process because life gets so hectic that I, too, become lax in following through on little things such as calling friends just to say "hello."

It is obvious to me that other regions throughout the United States do not think as we do. I have noticed that when I do these little things for people outside the South, they are completely thrown off guard by the gesture because they don't understand. Sometimes they're suspicious and wonder what my hidden agenda might be. When a Southerner does something nice for you, there isn't a hidden agenda. It is simply a reflection of a considerate upbringing that compares with no other.

Cindy became a good friend of mine because she is married to one of my best friends, Johnny. And, my goodness, what a good friend she is. You can always count on her. I called one day and asked if she would pick up a special-edition porcelain angel for my wonderful godmother, Mary Nell, who had done an extraordinarily nice favor for me (it takes a lot of people to keep me going). Mary Nell collects these angels from a store that is near Cindy's house, but quite a distance from me. Cindy picked it up, called, and said, "I'll meet you halfway and bring it to you. Just let me know when." Another hugely thoughtful thing to do. One day, I found that I was going to be near Cindy's and with no more than thirty minutes' notice, she arrived with both the angel and a warm loaf of bread, just out of the oven. *I'm* the one who should have been taking homemade bread to *her*!

Cindy's charm works well in keeping her husband happy and content because she tries very hard to be the best wife possible. We all went to the movies one night to see a rather gory war film, which we all (I thought) were anxious to see. During one of the particularly bloody battles, I glanced over to see Cindy with her eyes shut. Honestly, she must have kept her eyes shut through forty-five minutes of that movie. I realized that she had no desire to see that movie, but because her husband did, she gladly went along and never once complained. I was amazed by her generosity and completely impressed that she did not, in any way, dampen the pleasure of the evening for anyone else.

As we were leaving the theater, I punched her husband in the arm and whispered, "I hope you appreciate that woman."

"Ouch!" he whimpered. "I do! Now, don't hit me again." He's a romantic charmer himself.

The kind of charm that is prevalent among Southern women is about being thoughtful of others rather than being selfish. It is about being a good sport rather than a wet blanket.

Is a woman's charm deliberately manipulative? With some women, sometimes—yes. With Southern women, most of the time—no. Manipulation comes from the mind. Our charm comes from the heart. *Manipulation* is a word that we have come to dislike in today's society because we take it to mean control by evil methods. And, quite frankly, manipulation as we know it means that the manipulator usually wins and the one who is manipulated usually loses or, at best, gains no advantage. Southern women, on the other hand, scheme, plot, and charm to get the best results for everyone.

Typical Southern women are not manipulative. We are merely persuasive. We use our charm to gently bring the other party around to our way of thinking. We reason, cajole, flatter, flirt, whatever it takes. But we never give up, and therein lies the key to success. If you have ever split a log of wood (I haven't, but I'm really good at watching it done), you know that the log doesn't split with the first blow of the ax, or the second. It often takes several blows before it splinters into two pieces. It wasn't the last blow that did the job, but the combination of all the blows that fell before. That's how the charms of Southern women work. If it doesn't work the first time, we keep working until the resistance crumbles.

Here's how charm works for a typical Southern woman. I came close to missing a flight one day due to a stopped hotel clock and a short-circuited brain. I raced through the airport (of course, my flight was at the very last gate) and got there with three minutes to spare. I boarded the plane, only to sit there for over an hour and a half while mechanics worked on some problem. Finally, we departed, but it was not a comfortable flight. It was a cross-country trip, which normally calls for a roomy L1011, but this plane was so small that you had to turn sideways to walk down the aisle to THE rest room. Yep, it was a packed four-hour flight, and there was only one working rest room. It was not a pleasant day.

We landed and I, tired and weary, dragged myself to the baggage-claim area where I waited patiently for my luggage that never showed up on the conveyor belt. Normally, I would have been slightly or rather greatly annoyed by this point. However, my father had passed away two weeks earlier, and I was reminded of an important lesson: Irritating inconveniences are trivialities and should be treated as such. I approached a special customer-service representative. I was smiling and much more pleasant than any woman should have to be under such stressful circumstances.

"You look like *just* the person who can help me," I began in a jovial, flirtatious tone. I smiled broadly and, I hoped, enchantingly.

Immediately and visibly, he melted. Remember, these people get beat up all the time, so one kind word and they'll move mountains for you.

"Why, yes, ma'am, I certainly can. What is the problem?"

"My luggage did not arrive and since I live an hour from the airport, I'm sure you won't mind sending it by courier to me so that I don't have to drive all the way back down here." I stopped, smiled, and fluttered my eyelashes. "After all, it isn't *my* fault that the luggage isn't here."

"I'll be happy to do that for you. Come with me and we'll check on it."

We struck up a conversation and chatted quite amicably while he discovered the bag had made it from the West Coast, only to be put on a connecting flight. They scrambled quickly and got the suitcase off the plane and delivered it, soaking wet, to me (did I mention it was also raining and when I got to the parking lot, my car wouldn't start?). I thanked him and decided that things were going so well, I should try to get something for my efforts.

"Don't you have some upgrades or something you could give me for future flights?" I smiled deeply and again looked up through my eyelashes. "My goodness," I cooed flirtatiously. "It has been such an exasperating day. And you do have to admit that I have been quite a good sport about it all." I fluttered my eyelashes again.

He chuckled and reached in his jacket pocket and started pulling out all kinds of coupons for this and that. The coupons stuffed my billfold to the point that I could barely close it. With charm, I had solved a problem and then received compensation for my trouble. You might as well know that I am a big one for being compensated. It goes a long way toward alleviating my annoyance. I have discovered that companies are happy to be accommodating if you ask for something reasonable. If I have trouble with my phone, I ask for a deduction in my bill. One night I got home from grocery shopping to find that the clerk had left a bag out of my purchase. I was not happy when I drove all the way back to the store. When I got there, I sweetly suggested they give me that bag of groceries free of charge. They did.

When I left the airport that night, I gave the customer-service representative my card that had my e-mail address on it. The next morning I had an e-mail that began, "How's my favorite passenger? Last night, with all the rain, we had so many problems and, unfortunately, the others were not as nice about it as you were."

That young man and I are now wonderful friends because I responded to an annoying situation with charm. He mirrored my actions and treated me with charm and grace, too. And, on top of that, we both made a new friend.

Now, if you're a cynic of any kind, you have probably narrowed your eyes and are about to ask sarcastically, "Yes, but would that have worked if the airline clerk had been a woman?" Believe me, I've heard that question before.

Let me tell you—absolutely. Charm works as well with women as with men. Charm, don't forget, is merely a nice, kind way of treating others. On another trip, I stupidly left behind a beloved sweater in a hotel room. I called the front-desk clerk when I discovered that it was missing. Over the phone, I used charm and kindness, and the young woman went out of her way to find the sweater and mail back it to me. And, yes, you may say, "That's their job." Let me assure you, job or not when rushed or hassled, people can "pretend" to look rather than actually looking. When something is truly important to you, pull out all the stops to get it and use charm to your best advantage.

How do Southern women get what we want from the men in our lives? First of all, we rarely have to ask. Normally, we merely mention or suggest something and before you know it, it's ours. Want a new car? Here's how to do it:

Decide what you want and then every time you see it, comment on it to him. Look wistful. Finally—and don't get discouraged because men are really slow at this—he'll say, "You really like that car, don't you. You've mentioned it several times."

You shrug nonchalantly. "Yeah, it's a great car."

"You'd look wonderful in that car," he'll reply because, of course, you picked a sexy, hot style. You smile demurely and slide your arm through his, "That's so sweet. Thank you for saying that."

Then the lightbulb goes on. "Hey, why don't we buy you a car like that?" You looked stunned, shocked at such a statement. "What!" you barely gasp. "Why, honey, we can't afford that car!"

"Yes, we can," he'll reply. "And if you want it, we'll get it." Of course, you continue to protest over the next few days or even weeks. The more you protest, the more he'll want to buy that car for you and you can bet that he will. The key is patience and continuous gentle prodding. This is not manipulation because you are not controlling him or his thoughts. You're simply placing the thought in his mind, and we all know that we always like ideas much better when they're *our* ideas, not someone else's.

We remind our men constantly but sweetly that everything we do is for them. Because, usually it is. For instance:

"I bought this dress today because I know you love this color and style on me. Do you love it? If you don't, I'll take it back."

This should never be used as a bluff or empty gesture. I've said this many times and the few times that the outfit was disliked or met with a lukewarm response, I immediately took it back to the store. Without hesitation. I have never had any interest in wearing anything that the man in my life did not think was sensational. I want any man I am with to be proud to be my escort.

When you buy something special with him in mind, make certain he knows it.

"I bought these new pillows for you today. I know how much you love down pillows, and these are the best made!" Applying such tactics and thoughtfulness will assure you anything you want in life. Make him feel special, and he'll give you the world.

Southern women cleverly use their charms as precisely as a corporate sales department develops a strategic plan. Using charm in personal and professional relationships is easy when you remember to:

- Make life as pleasant as possible for those around you.
- Not argue over petty issues.
- Be flexible. Bend when necessary.
- Show support and encouragement for those around you.
- When a disturbing situation arises, sit down and discuss

it in a level tone and employ complete reason and logic. Being logical and reasonable means: Take to heart what the other person has to say. Carefully consider his position. Don't be selfish. Don't see only "your" side. Put yourself in the other's shoes.

- Be considerate and thoughtful.

Unfortunately, not every single Southern woman follows this behavior. I know a couple of women who rule with absolute dominance in their families. They are strong willed, selfish, demanding, and stop just short of using their brooms to beat their beleaguered husbands. And, it works. They get everything they want. Theirs is the final word in the household because no other words are allowed. But they enjoy a hollow victory. Secretly, they detest the men who allow them to dominate, while the men are miserable in an emotionally abusive marriage. Social acquaintances shun these couples because they feel uncomfortable being around a relationship that resembles that of a parent and child rather than a husband and wife.

Oh, what a little charm could do.

Regardless of what some might say, there is no surefire prescription that works every time for landing or keeping a husband. The same approach simply will not work on *every* man, especially highly successful ones. Southern women know that and we tailor our approach to the man, although some elements remain constant. The nonvariable elements are that we:

- Present ourselves as feminine, luscious creatures.
- Let him know that we are interested and available. Then,

wait for him to come to us. We don't chase but rather relax on a chintz-covered chaise until he comes to us. I once waited fifteen years for one guy to ask me out! In the South, women are still extremely uncomfortable with calling a man up and asking him on a date. When we meet someone who interests us, we'll press our business or personal card in his hand as we leave and say, "Please call me sometime for lunch. I'd love to continue this conversation." Or, if we find ourselves in possession of concert tickets that were a gift—never ones we purchased ourselves because that would be stretching it too far—we might invite a gentleman who has caught our fancy. As my friend Deb says, "If a man doesn't recognize a fine, well-bred woman when he meets one, then just let him date all the trash he wants!"

- Make him feel special and cherished.
- Accent his life with specialized touches such as preparing home-cooked meals and sewing buttons on his shirt (it's the easiest thing in the world to do).
- Learn more about his special interests and share them with him.
- Never become dependent and clingy—that scares a man in less time than it takes to make a bowl of instant grits. Of course, there is a fine line to toe because a man is also driven away by too much independence. He has to feel needed. It is important to find the proper balance.
- Don't go after him if he goes away. Let him come back on his own accord or let him stay gone. Sometimes, a man will become afraid of the feelings he develops when he meets a sensational woman, so he disappears for a while

to sort through those. For goodness sake, don't panic and pursue. You'll drive him further away.

The major variable in relationships is adapting to the man's lifestyle. Every woman, at some time or other, has dreamed of marrying a successful man and having a comfortable, even luxurious, life. Stop and think about it for a minute. What makes a man successful? Hard work and long hours. A man's success, coupled with a healthy financial statement, does not magically appear like a winning lottery ticket.

If a man is an entrepreneur, he rushes around like a crazed animal making phone calls and negotiating business deals. The pace of business has gotten worse over the last decade, thanks to the constant use of pagers, cell phones, fax machines, and laptop computers. Business is now a nonstop whirlwind of activity. How can you expect a man like that to remember to call by a certain day to ask for a date for the weekend? How could you possibly be upset when that kind of man is two days later in calling than he promised, when during the last forty-eight hours he has orchestrated a $10-million real estate deal or a $1 billion merger? How could you possibly be angry when his executive assistant calls and says, "Mr. Big Shot had to fly to Dallas on business today, but he wanted me to advise you that he will phone when he returns on Thursday."

In the South, we say, "If you can't run with the big dogs, stay on the porch with the puppies." If your goal is to marry a corporate CEO or mega-millionaire businessman, learn right now to adjust. Or, resign yourself to staying on the porch.

I speak from experience. In my wild and reckless youth, I always took the approach that a man should call promptly on schedule, arrive on time, and never change plans at the last minute. On all fingers and all toes, I cannot count the rich, powerful men I have discarded after one slight infringement of my silly, mindless, self-imposed rules. And, of course, those men did not miss me one iota because there were dozens of women waiting in line behind me (ever notice how women flock to the rich and influential?). Then I got wise and began to watch the successful Southern women who landed in long-term relationships, even marriages, with these kinds of men. Those women were, without fail, patient, easy to get along with, flexible, endearing, and always willing to rise to the challenge.

As my own life got busier and I scurried from airport to airport, appointment to appointment, frantically making cellular calls, answering voice mail, snail mail, e-mails, faxes (there are just too many ways to communicate these days), I got the full picture. Remember when we escaped the phones by getting in the car? Those were wonderful, quiet times that gave us the opportunity to slow down and remember things we needed to do and think about other people. No one has that time anymore, especially successful businesspeople. Antiquated rules from the 1930s, when life was much, much simpler, will not work in the frantic pace of the twenty-first century.

That is, they won't work if you want to capture a man with a high-earning capacity. It might work if you want to marry someone who works at a leisurely pace and earns only enough to keep you in store-brand jeans rather than drape you in Armani or Versace.

However, if a successful man is what you want, understand that you have to be ready and willing to come second on many occasions. Whatever it is that made him rich, famous, or both will come first. I have *never* seen an exception to this rule, so don't think you can change it. Accept him for what he is and go with it.

Charm that disarms this kind of successful man requires patience. It means that you look at the big picture rather than focusing on the instant photo. It insists that you roll with the punches rather than taking offense at each hit. It means that you adapt and swallow your pride from time to time.

It does not mean, however, that you can't draw some lines in the sand or that you allow a man to walk all over you. If a man stands you up or repeatedly breaks his word, have a nice, nonthreatening discussion with him. One that goes something like this:

"I realize that you're extremely busy and I try to acknowledge that and work with you. However, I am busy, too, and if we make plans, I have committed that time to you. Out of respect and courtesy, I think I am owed more consideration. Would you agree with that? Good. Now, how can we work this out where it works for both of us, because I would really like to do that."

Don't threaten. Don't issue ultimatums. Just talk it out reasonably and stand your ground sweetly. Don't forget that other beautiful, sexy women are waiting in line behind you should you choose to abort the mission.

Here's another valuable tip for landing the most eligible bachelor you know: Observe carefully what the other women are doing and then do the exact opposite. Obviously, what they're doing is not working, so do something different. My observation is that women literally throw themselves at these kinds of men. They're too aggressive, too eager, and then, when they gain some security in the relationship, are too demanding. Try the Southern approach of being the quintessential woman who is willing to adapt and adjust.

Remember that gently disarming the opponent with charm is always much more effective than using any other kind of ammunition.

CHAPTER THREE

SWEET AS VINEGAR PIE

SOUTHERN WOMEN have the sweetest way of saying the meanest things. It's a lot like those flavored cough syrups and liquid aspirins in which the medicine is beautifully disguised in a flow of sugary sweetness. Southern women can force a dose of medicine down your throat, and all the time you're thinking how good the sugar tastes—not how bitter the medicine is.

How do we do it? It's the one question that non-Southerners ask most frequently. It's very simple. You smother the bad stuff with lots of good stuff. It's similar to making a sweet, delectable dessert out of vinegar. In the 1800s and early 1900s, vinegar pie was one of the most popular desserts in Southern cuisine. It is made with a tiny amount of vinegar and a bunch of sugar. As the Depression years choked the mountains and backwoods of the South, it gained renewed popularity because the recipe could be made for pennies. To be quite truthful, it is a delicious example of how to turn something bitter into something extraordinarily sweet. And, it's a lot like a Southern woman—a little tartness completely enveloped in sweetness.

But back to the sugar-coated tongue lashings we're famous for in the South. Whenever there's bad news to be delivered in the form of a chewing out, there's always a lot of good that can be said, too. Unfortunately, people have come to think that bad goes with bad and good goes with good. In the South, we mix a whole heap of good with the bad. You can say anything you wish as long as you say it in a nonoffensive way. It's this simple: Make someone feel good about her positive attributes, then slip in comments about her negative ones. Many times, the person is so caught up in the compliments that it is much later before she realizes that she has been criticized. She even asks herself how you meant what you said. But, nonetheless, she takes notice and absorbs the criticism without getting mad.

I know someone who is the most self-destructive person I have ever met. He is professionally successful but a personal failure of sorts because he never manages to get control of his life. He will work very hard for months on the road to putting his happiness together. Then, within minutes, his impulsiveness ruins everything he has worked toward. He is like an alcoholic who resists a drink for months and then ruins everything by going on a binge.

In a phone conversation one day, he was grousing as usual after another impulsive splurge had gobbled up several steps of previous progress.

"You really amaze me," I said in an even tone. "You're one of the smartest people I have ever met. In fact, I've learned more from you than anyone else I've ever known."

On the other end of the phone, I knew that a smile was beginning to tug at the corners of his mouth.

"You will never know how grateful I am for the things I

have learned personally and professionally from such a sharp person," I continued matter-of-factly.

In my mind, I visualized that he was arrogantly tilting his chair back and the smile was getting much bigger.

"After all, you have an IQ of a hundred and fifty," I remarked. "You're practically a genius."

"Well, it's one forty-eight," he corrected in an attempt to be modest, but the tone was saturated with pride.

"What's two points?" I ask. "As I was saying, I am completely amazed by you."

"Thank you." He was close to giddiness at that point.

"What amazes me the most and puzzles me completely, though, is how someone who has so much intelligence, education, and common sense can do such stupid things to mess up his life. Can you explain that? After all, I'm not as smart as you and I need some explanation. It bewilders me." There was no sarcasm in my voice, only plaintive interest.

The smile, I knew, vanished and the pride evaporated. Yet, his ego had been so soothingly stroked that, without anger, he said very calmly, "That is a very good question and something I definitely need to put some thought into. You're right. I am smart, so why do I do these stupid things?"

I couldn't have said it better. But I didn't. He did.

I have a friend who asked for a divorce in the most beautiful, thoughtful way you can imagine. She and her husband sat down and she said, "We've tried so hard to make this work, and it just isn't working. You are a wonderful person and you deserve a happy marriage, not the one you've got. You're not happy, and I sadly realize that it's out of my power to make you happy. Obviously, I'm not the woman you can be happy with. You've brought me so much love and happiness, and I will never forget that. But, I think it's best for both of us, if we move on now while we're both still young enough to start over and one day find someone else. You deserve that, and I want that for you."

Both cried, shared happy remembrances, and agreed to a divorce that was completely free of acrimony. Never mind the fact that she strongly suspected he had a girlfriend. She made her point when she said, "Obviously, I'm not the woman you can be happy with." She was saying, in essence, you've made your choice. She took the high road and saved both of them a lot of additional heartbreak because they had struggled so long with the marriage. And because she made him feel good about himself—not rejected and discarded—he did not react with maliciousness.

My mother is perfectly trained at slipping in a criticism wrapped so beautifully in compliments that the negative words barely singe as they whiz by. She does it by chattering happily and amiably; then, in the same tone with no change in inflection whatsoever, she delivers the punch and segues flawlessly into another wonderful compliment. My mother is a dressmaker, so many customers, particularly brides and bridesmaids, have felt the sting of her honesty—especially as she takes their measurements. One bridesmaid laughingly tells the story of her first fitting when mother said:

"There are so many girls who would kill to have a beautiful bustline like yours. Honestly, you are very fortunate and you should realize that. You also have one of the *tiniest* waists I ever saw! It's your *butt* that's so big. Of course, it looks bigger because your waist is so small."

Just what every woman likes to hear—how large her rear end is. But, despite her honesty, everyone adores my mother and repeatedly turns to her for advice. The barbs are ignored because they are so charmingly and "innocently" delivered.

On the other hand, my paternal grandmother could have used some practical instruction in sugarcoating acid-tongued barbs. She was a nurse with ambitions too big for her small town, so she packed her dreams and prized hair combs and took a bus to a Northern land of opportunity. It was many years before she returned to the South, but when she did it was obvious that what little tact she had previously possessed had disappeared like cotton candy in a rainstorm. It sent the family into somewhat of an uproar because no one was accustomed to a woman who spoke her mind with utter bluntness. In fact, some called it "unrestrained brutality" and swore that life among the untamed pagans had destroyed the beautiful soul of a Southern lady. When, in fact, my grandmother had never had a soul that even *bordered* on beautiful and a "lady" was the last thing she wished to be called. My grandmother, decades ahead of the feminist movement, preferred to be known as a capable, independent *woman* who could chop wood and outshoot any man.

She could, indeed, shoot the center out of an apple from two hundred paces and rarely ventured far without her pistol packed in her purse. She was a big, rotund woman with beady eyes and had she not lived in the remote mountains of the Deep South, she surely would have had her own gang like Ma Barker.

Anyway, back to the story. When she returned from the North, there was never any way of telling what was going to come out of that woman's mouth. A visit to Mamaw's house was an adventure in itself, little of which had anything to do with the melt-in-your-mouth tea cakes for which she was famous. One day, she took a strong, appraising look at my scrawny eleven-year-old sister whose dark hair flopped around her head like a mop out of control. With no preamble, she unloaded the verbal buckshot that my sister claims scarred her for life.

"You're such an ugly little thing," she clucked, shaking her head with thinly veiled disgust. "Don't worry, though. *Maybe* you'll grow out of it."

The ugly duckling did, in fact, blossom into the most beautiful of swans and if her self-esteem *was* punctured by Mamaw's poisonous stickpin, you would never know it by the rousing success she made of her life.

Another favorite tactic of Southern women is to turn the blame on themselves while slathering the other person with goopy praise. We are more than happy to sacrifice our pride to get what we want or to save money. If you find yourself trapped in a contract for tango lessons that you signed in a moment of brain failure, try this approach:

"Without a doubt, you are the best tango instructor in the world. Far too superior to waste your talents on such a hopeless worm as I who, obviously, has two left feet. I know that we're only five lessons into a one hundred-lesson contract, but quite honestly, if we continue I'm afraid that I am going to ruin your business and your reputation. Although I am so grateful that you are sharing your glorious talent with me, I am afraid that I am only dragging you down. It isn't fair to you, so I realize that I need to get over my selfishness and do what's best for you."

Having problems at work with your boss or a co-worker? Do personalities clash constantly? Swallow your pride, make an honest list of the person's positive attributes (yes, everyone has at least some of them), and try this:

"Would you mind if we talk for a moment? I have a great

deal of admiration for you for so many reasons. You're a good manager, a thoughtful friend, and a wonderful father. You're very talented and creative. However, I seem to annoy you for whatever reason, and I know that it makes things difficult for both of us. I'm sure it's me and not anything you're doing wrong. Could you please tell me what I am doing wrong or what I can do to make things more pleasant for both of us? It's very important to me, and I want to do whatever's necessary to make that happen."

This works like a charm because even the meanest people are touched by such humility. They'll reach out to you, give you a fair chance, and things will improve significantly. One word of caution, though: If the person offers some criticism, be prepared for it and listen to it. If that happens, it would also be a good time to practice responding with your criticism beautifully coated in spun sugar.

The most important elements in firing steel bullets from a licorice gun are these:

Tone—This is crucial. Keep it cheerful, sweet, level, conversational, or perhaps teasing. Never angry, stern, condescending, or hateful. Remember, it's not what you say, it's how you say it.

Facial expression—Smile, or at least keep the corners of your mouth upturned. Look pleasant, kinda like the way your mother looked when she shoved spinach into your mouth. Never frown or knit your eyebrows. A pleasant facial expression also helps to control your tone.

Sugarcoat the message—Remember to always deliver the

criticism with a tasty, large portion of flattery. Say three nice things for every bad thing you have to say. Make the person realize that he/she or the situation has far more good than bad in it.

Southern women speak their minds, but often in a way that's spun with so much sugar it isn't offensive. Other times, they speak so disarmingly honestly and in such a level tone that people are taken aback and not quite sure of what has just been said, particularly when the statement is punctuated with a great big smile.

Many of television's best interviewers are Southern women who have the enviable and extraordinary knack of asking the toughest questions in the most charming way. Oprah Winfrey, Katie Couric, Deborah Norville, Diane Sawyer, Leeza Gibbons, and Phyllis George are amazing in their ability to ask hard, edgy questions in such a subtle, charming way that neither the interviewee nor the audience is uncomfortable when questions are asked. These are all terrific examples of Southern women who know how to be tough yet perfectly poised and feminine.

My favorite example is Katie Couric who, during an interview with a powerful, well-known CEO, asked the most difficult question possible. She delivered it as gracefully as if she had asked him to join her for lunch. Because the subject was so touchy, the CEO bristled and responded with prickly opposition. Immediately, she began giggling in that wonderfully girlish manner of hers that is so disarming and so completely enchanting.

"Okay, okay," she said laughing. "Would you agree that things are not as good as you would like?"

A brilliant move that immediately diffused the situation.

The CEO settled down, relaxed, and said, "Yes, I would agree." Then, he elaborated. A wonderful compromise that produced a win for both sides. Katie asked the tough question in a charming manner and got her answer. She was shrewd enough to realize that if she allowed the CEO to save face rather than drilling him harder, they would both emerge victorious. And, so they did.

I have friends who pal around with a guy who is, to put it kindly, abrasive. He is argumentative and contrary, but somewhere hidden in the brusque demeanor are some redeeming qualities. I think.

Anyway, this guy, Rick, stopped by to see Jimmy, another friend of mine one day. Jimmy's grandmother, Nano, lived with the family and she answered the door. She peered suspiciously through the screen door at the large, bearded creature lurking on the front porch.

"Hello, Mrs. Cain!" Rick greeted her in his best Eddie Haskell impersonation. "I'm Jimmy's friend, Rick. Do you know who I am?"

A deep furrow appeared in her brow as her mind and eyes searched for a clue as to who the stranger was. Suddenly, her face brightened like the sun dawning on a beautiful new day.

"Oh yes, I know who you are! Please come in," she exclaimed, beaming sweetly from ear to ear as she pushed the door open to welcome him. "*You're* the one they call *obnoxious!*"

That's Nano—sweet as vinegar pie.

CHAPTER FOUR

If Life Were Fair, Pecan Pie Would Have No Calories

If life were fair, a grown and otherwise sophisticated woman like me would not have the freckles of a six-year-old and the dimpled thighs of a sixty-year-old.

Do you see any fairness in that?

Why is it that some things from our youth such as freckles refuse to vanish while those supple, smooth thighs (which we didn't even realize we had at the time, so we couldn't appropriately appreciate them) segue into cellulite upon the arrival of the big two-one and certainly no later than the age of twenty-five?

Life is not fair. Of this, I am certain. If it were fair, I would be several inches taller like the rest of my family and have the same beautiful, perfectly pointed nose that they all possess rather than the small, pug one that hangs somewhat lopsided on my face. And, that scrumptious pie made with pecans, sugar, and syrup as thick as an Alabama accent would have no calories.

No, life is not fair. For men or women. But for women, it is often more emotionally battering because of the extra sensitivity we possess—that special awareness that makes us compassionate, tenderly loving, and thoughtful. That special sensitivity that makes us gentle lovers, caring friends, and loving mothers.

The depth of our emotions make us wonderful and warm, yet the same emotional depth can make us tortured souls who struggle with life's difficulties. Our sensitivity is a two-edged sword. It pierces our hearts like Cupid's arrow so that we can feel great romantic love for someone and experience ecstasy. We loooovvvveee that side of sensitivity.

What we don't love is when that same sensitivity acts as our enemy and the sweet tip of Cupid's arrow becomes a brutal butcher knife that carves apart our hearts with life's agonies. Finding a way to savor the sweetness that sensitivity brings yet avoid the bitterness is tricky business.

But Southern women know how to do it.

We Southern women know that the key to happy, balanced, fulfilled lives is to nurture those sensitive emotions that enhance our charm and compassion, yet draw the line firmly when those emotions threaten to deeply wound us.

Southern mothers prepare their daughters for life's unfairness at an early age. A mother may even whisper to the fair-haired child suckling at her breast, "Life will not be easy, sweet one. You must grow up to be strong and know how to take care of yourself. But, above all, you must always be a lady."

Honestly, I don't think my mother waited until I was nestled at her breast. She has harped on this for so long that I am convinced that she started my instruction while I was still in the womb.

To survive, we often have to dig in our perfectly manicured nails, kick off our high heels, and climb out of the dark hole without even the offer of a gentlemanly hand. But we do it. And traditional, well-bred Southern women do it gracefully and without complaint.

In this life, we have two choices when adversity clouds our skies—to be bitter or to be better. Being bitter will choke the joy from our lives and darken our days spent on earth. Choosing to be better after our troubling experiences, however, will enrich our days and add peace and contentment to our lives.

Southern women know to accept that life is neither a fairy tale nor fair and get on with the task at hand.

Bitter people are tortured individuals who are crippled emotionally from the raging anger that boils within their souls. This anger stifles happy, optimistic hope for the future. Bitter people become prisoners of their own sour attitudes.

Better people greet life's potholes of mishap and disaster with determination and, once the obstacle has been cleared, are philosophical and often reflective as a result of the occurrence, gleaning knowledge and education from it. Better people prosper in life; bitter people do not. Always choose to be better.

We Southern women realize that while we must control our hearts' reactions, it is critical not to build stone walls around our hearts. Some women would prefer to feel nothing at all, rather than subject themselves to the possibility of future anguish. This is a natural reaction, a normal defense for women who have been extremely hurt. But such a precaution causes further destruction because it destroys a loving, giving, cheerful heart. Captivating charm and charisma, the essence of perfect femininity, vanish, too, when a loving heart is shrouded with distrust and suspicion.

So, Southern women totter along a fine line, balancing precariously on a bridge that spans a heart divided into two parts. One side of the heart is wise and cautious, a throbbing chamber of knowledge created through painful experience. The other side, however, is a treasure chest filled with unsuspicious love, compassion, and an eternal belief that at the core of all people lies an innate goodness.

One side of the divided heart cannot exist without the other. Not if a woman is to survive the heartbreaks of life while maintaining an open, loving heart from which springs life-sustaining optimism. Not if she is to protect herself from unnecessary cruelties while still inhaling fully the sweetness that life offers.

Southern women are often called iron butterflies or steel magnolias because a hurricane of hurt or a tornado of emotional havoc cannot harm these indestructible females. Why? Simple. We Southern women can throw a shield of impenetrable protection around our soft hearts quicker than Tennessee Williams could down a bottle of wine.

We batten down the hatches and relegate our sensitivity to the darkest corners of our hearts. Fort Knox (located, incidentally and appropriately, in the South) would be easier to penetrate that a Southern woman's heart when a full-press defense is in play. The ability to pull such a maneuver is a well-kept secret of what appears to others to be a paradoxical combination of warm charm and formidable strength.

The bottom line is that we normally care deeply, but when our emotional survival is at risk, the entrance to our sensitivity slams shut like a steel trapdoor. A Southern woman is a chameleon who can metamorphose quickly from a steamy hot cup of spiced tea to a chilling glass of iced mint tea. Whatever the circumstances call for, that's what we do. That's how we survive without becoming cold and distant.

Southern women, after many years of discipline and training, develop the coveted skill of switching our emotions on and off. Some women, however, choose to shut off all feelings completely. These women become cold, distant, and completely unfeeling—which is quite unappealing to men, who desire softness and sensitivity from the opposite sex. Sensitivity, it goes without saying, is the underlying foundation of sensuality, and you know what an important function that sensuality performs! Still, some women throw away this womanly trait as easily as Southern women throw out burned fried green tomatoes.

Yes, these women survive quite well with this self-sufficient behavior. But they do not *enjoy* life. They *endure* it. Southern women, on the other hand, balance sensitivity with defensive detachment. We absorb and enjoy the sweet times in life and stoically endure the more difficult ones.

It's an uncomplicated matter of heart over mind. We *will* ourselves not to allow our hearts to be foolishly hurt. We depend on our womanly intuition to steer us away from the wrong people. A woman's instinct is her greatest ally. Follow that instinct, and you'll never go wrong. You'll weather the roughest storms in life.

Don't close off your feelings. Cutting off the ability to experience a wide range of emotions is similar to cutting off your nose to avoid the obnoxious smells in life. Okay, so you *won't* smell the stinky garbage, but is it worth missing the scent of those heavenly gardenias? NO!

You can have the best of all worlds by doing what we Southern women do—cherish deep feelings because they are necessary for a full, ebullient life yet realize that sometimes it is crucial to build a fortress around your soft heart.

Be pragmatic. Realize and accept that everyone is not special and considerate and that other people just don't think of the same thoughtful things you do. The first rule in protecting a sensitive, caring heart from harm: Don't expect too much, especially from those who give so little.

When life isn't fair, don't dwell on it. Move on. Ask yourself, "Will this matter tomorrow? Or in a month? Six months from now, will I even remember that I had this problem? Is it big enough to warrant such upset and distract me from even a few minutes of peace and happiness in life?" Probably not.

Protect your mind from negativity overkill. Southern women are ingenious at finding ways to push unpleasant thoughts from their minds. It is absolutely critical if you are to maintain a bright outlook and a high level of positive energy.

I have one friend who waits until April fifteenth every year to think about her taxes. Usually, she files for an extension.

"Why do you always do this?" I asked in the imperious tone of someone who files weeks early.

"Why not?" she asked with a shrug. "I always have to pay and if I paid in February and then I died before April fifteenth, it would have been a waste of time, money, and worry."

See how brilliant Southern women can be?

Southern women focus on keeping their priorities straight when the road of life takes those crooked turns. Family—the backbone of the tradition that holds their culture together—is tremendously important to the women of the South. We believe that people, not possessions and money, are important. Jobs and salaries can be replaced; lives cannot.

A few years ago, I was at a very difficult place in my life—or so I thought. Almost simultaneously, I went through a sad divorce, corporate downsizing, and other very hurtful events. Nothing seemed to be going right. Then, I learned that my dad was terminally ill.

That's when everything was put into perspective very quickly.

I left the hospital one night in tears. When I got home, I sat down and made a list of the worst things that could happen to me—things that I could not repair and that would be extremely difficult, if not impossible, to overcome. I was amazed to discover that the things I had previously been upset over ranked way down my list. In fact, none of those things ranked higher than twentieth!

For an agonizing time, I had my problems in the wrong order of importance. I was personally responsible for my own torment. I was raised better than that (one of my mother's favorite admonishments) and knew differently, but the onslaught of so many problems at once had given me temporary amnesia. It happens to everyone at one time or another.

Try this exercise when problems mount in your life: Is the loss of your job worse than the death of a loved one? No way! Is a divorce more devastating than the loss of your eyesight or hearing? Absolutely not! Would you prefer the loss of your good health forever to that suffocating debt you're facing? Never in a hundred years! Southern women know that the best way to survive and enjoy life is to put things into proper perspective.

Southern fathers have a great deal to do with the independence that is instilled in their daughters. While they love and cherish their daughters, they know that the best way to prepare them for the unfairness of life is to teach them to be self-reliant.

My father, the original Mr.-Black-and-White-Never-Any-Gray-Areas, used to lecture his daughters on proper divorce settlements.

"You can get married and if it doesn't work out, you're always welcome to come back home," he would say in a kind voice before dropping the hammer. "But you'll come home with exactly what you left with and what you worked to earn while you were gone and not one penny more. You won't take the poor boy for all he's got. And, I'm here to see to that."

Daddy was determined that his Southern daughters wouldn't contribute to the unfairness of life for anyone else.

I would like to say that I was only *slightly* rather than *greatly* embarrassed when I learned that Daddy had called my divorce attorney to ascertain that his commandment was being followed and that I was not taking more than my fair share in my divorce settlement.

My attorney, a very dear, wonderful family friend, assured Daddy that the lesson had taken hold and he would be very proud of the way I had handled everything.

"She is certainly your daughter," Jim told him. "She stresses absolute fairness in everything she does."

"Gee, I'm glad I didn't try anything underhanded," I mumbled, slumping down in my chair when I heard this story. "I never dreamed of him calling to check up on me. After all, I did pass the age of legal consent many years ago."

Yet, Daddy was right. Life may not always be fair to us,

but *we* can always be fair to others. He also knew something else very important: taking more than my fair share would not have been a declaration of my independence. It would have been an extension of dependence. Southern women are fiercely proud and doggedly independent.

When I was sixteen, I had a slight fender bender and was beyond consolation by the time my dad arrived. I was convinced that my fledgling driving career was over before it had barely begun.

"Why are you crying?" he asked.

"Look what I've done!" I bawled, pointing to a bashed quarter panel. My father, normally a strict disciplinarian, used love and understanding that day to teach me one of the greatest lessons of my life. He put his arm around my shoulders.

"Don't ever worry about anything that money and hard work can replace," he said. "Save that worry for the times when hard work can't replace what you've lost."

Many times when I've suffered a financial setback, I have remembered that advice and I think how I would rather lose money than my health or a member of my family. Our minds are the most important fiber of our being. Never underestimate the mind's power to deliver us into success or drop-kick us into despair. As we believe, so shall it be.

Life is not always fair, but it does reward a positive, won't-quit attitude. Southern women adjust to the unfairness of life by making our own breaks rather than allowing life to break our spirits. Just like everyone else, we encounter sourness in circumstances but we smother it with sugary sweetness and make it palatable.

Here's a trick we use in dealing with those emotionally wrenching times: Force positive thoughts into your head and talk positively to yourself even when your heart's not in it. Mull it over and wonder what good things will evolve from the unpleasant situation. Repeat over and over phrases like "Good will come from this. Good will definitely come."

And good always *does* come. Many times, our greatest blessings in life are delivered by way of disruptive, unhappy times. Without trials and tribulations, we would not have the triumphs.

Just remember:

You won't always get a fair break. Sometimes you'll get painful breaks, but many times you'll find you were solely responsible for making your own lucky breaks or orchestrating the breaks that turned things around for you.

Train yourself to tackle obstacles, not avoid them. You gain strength and greater independence every time you defeat an intimidating situation—the kind of situation that makes you want to turn and run but, instead, you stay and fight. Southern women are trained from childhood to confront and conquer difficult circumstances. Consequently, we become the sturdy backbone of our homes.

Don't depend on a man to sweep you away and make your life's troubles disappear. And, if you don't have that man, don't spend your life dreaming of a man who can do that. You have as much power as a man has—even more when it comes to your own life. Do it yourself.

Don't whine and complain. Accept life's heartbreaks and

disappointments and learn from them. Regardless of how bad things are for you, they could be worse.

Reflect with gratitude rather than with regret or bitterness. Be thankful for the hard times, the lessons you learn, and the beautiful destinations to which the hard times and lessons lead.

Southern women are not bystanders in life. We are avid participants who grab destiny by the neck and choke the life we want out of it. We are undaunted by unfairness. We simply climb back onto the diving board and plunge into the cold waters of uncertainty, certain only that adventure of some kind lies ahead.

Life's not fair. So what? I discovered that when I was eleven and found that my favorite foods were making me pudgy and that the handsome, dark-haired object of my affection loved the beautiful, exotic Pamela while the red-haired, freckled one with crooked teeth adored me. But life *is* manageable and it can be lots of fun—particularly when handled with skill and a positive outlook.

But for those times when life is disgustingly hard, try a little Southern comfort food. And what sweeter indulgence than a decadent pecan pie?

GEORGIA PECAN PIE

¾ cup sugar
¾ cup white Karo syrup
3 beaten eggs
1 teaspoon vanilla
Dash of salt
1 cup chopped pecans
3 tablespoons butter
2 tablespoons flour

Mix and beat all ingredients together. Pour into 9-inch deep-dish pie shell. Bake at 350 degrees for 50 minutes.

It's got a few calories, but you just never mind those, you hear? Believe me, sweetheart, it is *worth* it!

CHAPTER FIVE

PRETTY IS AS PRETTY DOES

"Pretty is as pretty does," my mother often chanted (which is a nice way of saying "harped on continually"). I wish I had a dime for every time I heard this saying and a dollar for every time it was followed by a lengthy lecture. With that kind of money, I would already be retired. In fact, I would just have skipped college and gone straight to the beach.

Mother was trying hard to do her proper maternal duties since I was a somewhat chubby child with lots of freckles and crooked teeth and it certainly seemed that inward beauty was much more of a possibility than outward beauty. She was working diligently to build the self-esteem of an ugly duckling by emphasizing that beauty that radiates from the inside will turn even the plainest women into fabulous beauties. And, of course, as mothers often are, she was right. She was also determined to instill, or rather *embed,* in me the gracious, kind manners of a proper Southern lady. Southern women know what many women have forgotten—that character and spirit are the true beauty of a woman. A vibrant spirit and strong character radiate a breathtaking beauty that cannot be created by a perfect profile, orthodontics, cosmetics, or plastic surgery (not that we're opposed to any of that!).

Southerners are raised to be excruciatingly polite and considerate. We keep drawers full of notepaper for those endless thank-you notes, end every request with please (dear husband, may we have sex tonight, please?), and address our elders with "ma'am" and "sir" until the day we die. We overapologize, practice etiquette, and study every situation carefully to determine the appropriate amount of thoughtfulness to be applied.

When a friend or acquaintance dies, we bake cakes, cook casseroles, and rush to the funeral home in droves to pay our respects. My sister is quite adept at this routine, particularly the funeral home visits. The only requirement for her presence at a wake is that she at least know someone who knows someone who is distantly related to the deceased! She is such a frequent visitor that the funeral home in her small town has honored her with her own VIP parking space close to the front entrance!

In fact, she takes her duty so seriously (I'm *certain* it's duty and not nosiness) that she receives daily bulletins from the county coroner, who also happens to own the most popular funeral home in town. Ricky calls to tell her who's dead, whose body has just arrived, and who is clinging to life with a white-knuckled grasp that is weakening rapidly by the moment.

Okay, so maybe we go too far too often. But what's wrong with excess kindness and consideration? Today's world is often filled with extreme rudeness, so as far as I can see, the rest of the nation would benefit from adapting the gracious manners of a proper Southerner. Being kind and thoughtful enhances your own opinion of yourself because just as mother knew, it does build self-esteem. It also enables you to get much more of what you want out of life. How? People mirror our treatment of them. Thoughtfulness is matched by thoughtfulness, rudeness by rudeness, indifference by indifference. How we treat others is how we can expect to be treated in return.

Good manners lead us down the sugar-coated path to bending the rules. A store clerk who is treated with respect and politeness becomes willing to issue a refund forty-five days after a purchase, although the store rules say thirty days. A bank teller readily removes a late charge from your mortgage payment when you contritely and nicely explain you were on vacation and forgot to mail it. "Ma'am, I readily admit it was my fault, but it is the first time I have ever been late. Could you please consider taking off the late charge?" Employees in these positions have more power than you might sometimes imagine, but most important, they adore being treated with respect especially because they often receive abuse.

One evening I was having dinner with four female members of my family and I watched with interest as each of these Southern women ladled oozing charm on restaurant employees, including the busboy. They made everyone feel important and, as a result, we got extremely attentive service. There had been problems earlier, however, with an extremely long wait for a table in a half-empty restaurant and later with the food. The waitress offered to send over the manager.

"Oh, but honey, it's not your fault," chorused the women around the table. "You've done a great job." The spirits of a tired woman who had been on her feet for twelve hours visibly lifted and she responded with a weary, appreciative smile. When the manager appeared, I explained the problems in a nonangry tone. I began by smiling and then saying, "We haven't had a very pleasant dining experience tonight, and here's why." I kept my tone even but often sympathetic to how difficult his job might be. I ended by saying, "As you can tell, it's been a little frustrating and I thought you might like to know."

The manager, who had been nodding and quite attentive, replied, "Yes, ma'am, I understand and everything you said is absolutely correct." He went on to explain the labor, mechanical, and food problems he had had that day and then concluded by saying, "I apologize and I would like to make this up to you because I want you to come back and dine with us again." When the bill arrived, he had reduced the total by 50 percent! As we left, I walked over, shook hands with him, looked him directly in the eye, and said, "Thank you so much for what you did. It was very kind and it is very appreciated."

That's an important part of what Southern women know that every woman should know—thoughtful manners and kindness can turn any circumstance into a winning situation. Too often, we're tempted to think only of how things affect or inconvenience us with no consideration for the other side, such as the waitress who was forced unexpectedly to work a double shift or the manager who had encountered nothing but problems all day. Thankfully, good manners are never out of date.

I knew a non-Southerner, who lived for a while in the South, who was appalling in her lack of Southern hospitality. And, worse, she refused to learn. She hosted a "ladies" luncheon at an expensive restaurant for a departing executive and mailed invitations to several women who had worked closely with him. When the check arrived, she paid for herself and the guest of honor, then passed it around the table so that each "guest" could pay her share. We were stunned, speechless, and appalled! Nothing we had ever seen was as distasteful as that! That was years ago, and we're *still* talking about the time that ten well-bred, well-mannered Southern ladies were invited to luncheon by an outsider who didn't have the good breeding to pick up the check. It was a travesty of the worst kind.

Manners reveal true character. They are the greatest indicator of the heart that lies within. Kindness and consideration demonstrate a humble spirit while rudeness, if only momentary (and we all have those moments), is indicative of a haughty, better-than-thou belief. I know a man who shows sycophantic respect and courtesy to influential people who can help him either personally or professionally. To others, he is arrogant, belittling, and dismissive. But he fools no one, including the powerful and influential folks he most wants to impress. Everyone knows what kind of person he truly is, which tremendously diminishes *his* influence.

Using thoughtfulness and consideration in the workplace will take you further than anything else—including sixty-hour work weeks. Southern women discovered quickly when they entered the professional world en masse that using their social skills and manners worked as well at the office as at the country club. It was a natural transition to treat co-workers and bosses as nicely as if they were next-door neighbors. We Southern women treat bosses with as much thoughtfulness as we treat our best friends. We send a note of gratitude for a promotion or raise. When we see a book on a subject dear to the boss's heart, we buy it without hesitation and either without reason or for a special occasion.

A gracious Southern woman will buy a small "cheer up" gift for the receptionist who is in despair over her divorce. She takes a co-worker to lunch to show her appreciation for help on that big project. She sends endless handwritten notes throughout the company to congratulate others on promotions, weddings, or births. She clips magazine articles of interest to the CEO and sends them with a note that says simply, "Thought you might enjoy." Because she is so thoughtful and well mannered, her name is on the tip of every employee's tongue from the receptionist to the CEO. Her goodwill, which spreads cheer throughout the organization, also builds her reputation and increases her name recognition. Thoughtfulness and politeness are the best kinds of public relations. A high-profile, visible person gets promoted quicker than the quiet mouse in the corner cubicle who never squeaks, even if the mouse has an IQ of 160 and invented the first "people trap" that doesn't require cheese.

Southern women know the importance of treating security guards, parking attendants, maintenance workers, clerks, and others with as much respect as the chairman receives. We know that these people can often help us when the highest powers cannot or will not. If they are treated with courtesy, they will run, not walk, to the rescue.

It is also important to remember that people's stations in life can change quickly and what they are today may not be what they will be in five or ten years. A young man bagging groceries may one day reign as chairman and CEO over a huge global company like Coca-Cola, which is exactly what happened to Doug Ivester. In the South, we like to say, "Be careful whose toes you step on because they might one day be attached to the feet you have to kiss!"

I once worked in a fairly large organization that, like all modern corporations, depended heavily on computer technology. And since computer systems can be problematic in a large company, the technical-support group was always strung out and several days behind in fulfilling requests (actually, they were usually desperate *demands* rather than requests). I befriended all the technicians as well as the head of the department. I would call for no reason to leave cheerful messages or send a note of appreciation when they helped me in a pinch. I even sent a letter to the group vice president of the division to praise the technical-support department. As a result, my problems always got immediate attention, even when there were several jobs in front of mine.

On the other hand, another woman in my division treated the technical department with insouciant disregard and often disrespect. She never asked. She demanded. Her research job was dependent on a complex new computer system that had been delivered but not installed. The technical department was obviously dragging its feet. After six weeks of waiting, screaming, and threatening, she called every person of any importance in the company and launched into a barrage of insults against the tech area. This tactic resulted in further stalling.

One day my computer froze and so did I since I was on an urgent deadline (you know how those things always happen at the worst possible time). I called my buddies in the tech-support area. When Jorge answered, I began to sweetly serenade him.

"I love you Jorge. I really do. I love you Jorge. I do. I do," I squeaked in the voice that got me kicked out of the church choir. Jorge began to laugh and in an immediate attempt to cut off the squealing, he said in his heavy accent, "Okey. Okey. I be right over."

A few minutes later, Jorge had crawled under my desk and was working on the hard drive when Miss No-Manners-At-All from down the hall stormed into my office. "When did you call tech support for help?" she demanded with a narrow-eyed look.

I leaned back in my chair and smiled sweetly. "About fifteen minutes ago."

"Fifteen minutes ago! Are you serious?" she exploded.

"Actually, to be perfectly correct, I think it was more like *ten* minutes ago."

That made her even madder and like an old wet hen, she flew at Jorge and berated him and his entire department for making her wait weeks to install equipment that was absolutely essential to the success of the entire company. Jorge, who is from South America and is used to hot tempers, listened patiently until she finished with "What am I going to have to do to get my equipment installed?"

He stood up, dusted off his hands, shook his head slightly, and said quietly, "All you ever had to do was *ask nicely.*"

We Southern women realize that our greatest and most important beauty comes from within. That is why we work as diligently on our manners as we do on our bodies at the gym. Here are some ways that you can develop that inner glow:

Think positive, friendly thoughts. It shows on your face and makes you appealing and attractive. That glow, like a magnet, draws people to you.

Make a practice of carrying a slight smile on your face. No turned-down corners on your mouth—even when you're sitting at your computer, reading a book, or watching TV. As we grow older, our faces settle into position—let yours be settled in a turned-up smile.

Think kindly of others. Give them the benefit of the doubt. Force yourself to do this, even when it's not easy.

Be considerate and thoughtful. Good manners, or lack of them, reveal our true character. Be punctual and always honor your commitments. Arriving late for an appointment or breaking a promise demonstrates a lack of character *and* good manners.

Professionally and personally, send thank-you notes or small gifts of appreciation. Do something nice for someone for no reason at all. You'll feel better about yourself, and they'll never forget what you did. People react to us by mirroring our treatment of them—good or bad.

Take the time to carry a heavy package for an elderly person or to visit someone who is ill. Bring several magazines to a friend who is sitting at the bedside of a hospital patient. Time is the most important thing we can give, but it is always the one thing we hate to part with the most.

Place a call to someone who is going through the breakup of a relationship. Say nothing more than "I'm here if you need me." No need for discussion or meddling. Just be a friend.

Remember people during their times of heartbreak. Send flowers to a friend or co-worker on the day that her divorce is final. Be generous and thoughtful to others in their time of need. Give of yourself, and remember that often your time is more valuable and important to others than money.

Write a note or card of encouragement to someone who is experiencing difficult times. Relate a similar experience and how well it turned out for you.

Lend your best dress to your best friend. Then laugh if she ruins it. Money can replace dresses, but not friends.

Learn to bake cookies. Homemade goodies are the ultimate in graciousness and thoughtfulness.

Make time for your parents. Even when you don't have the time—the time will come when you wish you had.

Always say "please," "thank you," "yes, ma'am," "no, sir." Respect is not old-fashioned. I even find myself saying "Yes, ma'am" to sixteen-year-old salesclerks.

Open the door for someone (in the South, a proper lady *never* opens her own door!). Then, look the person directly in the eye and smile.

Speak kindly and with courtesy to everyone. From corporate CEOs to acquaintances to doormen to waitresses, everyone reacts positively to kindness.

Never impose or intrude on others. Be considerate of their time. Never ask of anyone what you would not be willing to give.

Don't gossip. It is indelicate and unladylike behavior.

Remember birthdays and anniversaries. For family, friends, neighbors, secretaries, co-workers. A simple call means as much as a card or elaborate gift. Especially when it's someone who doesn't expect you to remember that special day.

By behaving with good manners and graciousness, you will help to make the world a kinder, gentler place, but you will also be rewarded with success in both small and large ways. Habitual courtesy will deliver unto you untold rewards personally and professionally. You will have success you would not have achieved without excessive kindness and thoughtfulness. After all, if pretty is as pretty does then ugly is as ugly does. And everyone *always* likes "pretty" better.

Just ask any Southern mother.

CHAPTER SIX

Always Look Your Best Even If You Feel Your Worst

If pretty is as pretty does, then lovely is as lovely looks. We women of the South have what other women sometimes think is an obsession with our looks. It isn't necessarily our looks that concern us—it's our appearance.

Heart-stopping beauty complete with perfect noses, luscious lips, high cheekbones, and devastatingly sexy eyes aren't necessary to quench the thirst of our vanities. What *is* essential is to make the most of what we have and to always look our very best despite those cruel flaws that choke the shallow breath from desired perfection. It isn't a haughty vanity that permeates the soul of a Southern woman; it is, instead, an upbringing that demands meticulous attention to detail. If you must have a label for it, then call it "pride." Because of all the deadly sins known to woman, it is this one of which we Southern women possess an overabundance.

It is a phenomenon that is difficult, in fact downright

impossible, to explain that Southern women grow *more,* not less, concerned with appearance as their age increases. My mother, now many years into her monthly scrimpy dribble of social security checks, has never ceased to care how she looks. In fact, she grows increasingly fastidious with each year that is added to her biological calendar. There are few times, if ever, when I stop by to pick her up for church, a luncheon, shopping, or some other social gathering that she doesn't parade, swirl, or flitter for critique and approval.

"How does this look?" she asks. "Now, tell me the truth."

"You look fine," I reply with all the patience of a saintly daughter, barely glancing at her ensemble. "Now, come on. Let's go."

"Do I really?"

"Yes."

"What about these ear bobs? Do they match?"

"Your earrings are perfect. Would you please come *on?*" My patience strains, and the saintliness for which I am renowned begins to disperse into hundreds of tiny particles beyond my collective grasp.

"What about my hose? Are they the right shade? I really want to look pretty."

"Mother!" I erupt, my nomination for sainthood now gone with the wind. "We are going to be late! Get in the car! PLEASE!"

Then, one day I made the mistake of going one comment too far. "Mother, why are you so worried about it? You are too *old* to care this much about how you look."

No bullet could have found a more direct path to the center of her heart than those cold words fired by a trigger-happy tongue. Her shattered expression told that I had yet again disappointed her, so I fidgeted anxiously as I awaited the lecture that always begins with "No child has ever had a better mother than the one you've had or known more love. And to think that a child of mine would grow up to say such things to me just breaks my heart. It's *more* than I can *stand*."

But she didn't. Instead, she straightened further her almost perfect posture, arched an eyebrow, pointed that slightly crooked forefinger at me, and said, "Until the day I die, I will care how I look. Your daddy took great pride in how I took care of myself, and so I do. That doesn't change with age. In fact, I care more today than ever. And, if you have one ounce of me in you, when you're seventy years old, you'll care this much too."

She practices what she preaches. Always. Even under the most extraordinary conditions. A short time before her recent heart surgery, she was appropriately beautifying herself before she left her room for the procedure. I walked into the intensive-care unit to discover mother sitting up spryly in the bed while my sister coifed her hair to perfection. When she saw me, her face lit up radiantly, a gesture guaranteed to warm any daughter's heart.

"I'm so glad you're here," she bubbled with a beaming smile. My heart melted further.

"You're so sweet," I cooed.

"I need you to get my pocketbook for me," she instructed, ignoring my sentiment. "I need my lipstick and powder."

My warm glow evaporated as quickly as a flickering lightbulb that had suddenly lost its wattage.

"*What* are you doing?" I asked in a suddenly icy tone.

"I'm getting ready to go for my surgery," she answered brightly and in the same tone she would have used if the word "surgery" had been substituted for "party."

"Mother, you do not go to all this cosmetic trouble for surgery!" I admonished.

She waved my words away with a dismissive gesture. "It's important to look pretty when you go to surgery." She turned to my sister, who she knew would be an enthusiastic ally to support her cause. "Isn't that right?"

My sister nodded vigorously. "Yes, it is," she replied firmly. I must stop here to add that my sister should know, since she has had at least half of the surgeries known to the medical profession. So, in addition to funerals and funeral homes, she is also quite an expert on the etiquette of surgery.

"I *always* make up and look my best before *I* go into surgery," my sister continued. "*And,* I *never* allow them to put that ugly green cap on me *before* I get to the operating room. No sir! No way am I going to be rolled through the hospital corridors wearing that hideous thing where people can gawk at me!"

This is particularly understandable being as my sister always arranges for a large constituent of friends and family to line the halls of the hospital to wave sweetly and call out words of support as she is rolled toward the operating room. It looks amazingly like a parade route, and the bed is her float upon which she rides majestically toward her anesthetic destination.

In the South, looks aren't everything, but they're a big part of something we call "pride." Yet, my mother is absolutely right. I know many aging Southern women with the same unyielding commitment and some younger Southern women who could learn from their proud examples. I remember vividly a delicate Southern woman who, well into her eighties, paraded her perfectly prepared body down the aisle of the First Baptist church every Sunday morning. About twenty minutes before the sermon ended, the double doors in the back of the church would swing open ceremoniously and the bone-thin woman with red hair the color of her youth would totter in, wearing a snug-fitting, long, straight skirt and three-inch-high heels. The straightness of the skirt and the precariousness of the heels gave her a swagger, in fact a wiggle, that few twenty-year-olds would have had the agility to duplicate.

She was certainly a sight to behold and a treasure to appreciate. She graciously refused to be a relic but, instead, fashioned herself into a highly polished, well-maintained antique, more beautiful in the latter years of her life than in the dewy ones of her youth. I just never could figure out why she was always so late for church, and then I decided it was for one of two reasons. Either it takes a lot longer to make yourself look that good when you're that old or, more probably, she had already heard each sermon at least five or six times before and there just wasn't, quite frankly, anything new she could hear. My friend, Karen, however, subscribes to another theory. She steadfastly maintains that the woman was cleverly staging a showy entrance at a time when she was certain to be noticed by the entire congregation.

"Why do you think that?" I asked after yet another debate on the subject.

"*Because she's a Southern woman,*" Karen explained firmly. "There's not a Southern woman I know who doesn't like to be noticed. And the good Lord knows that we Southern women are absolutely in hog heaven when we're the *center* of attention. I have to hand it to her—that woman knew how to make herself the center of attention *every* Sunday."

Today's Southern women are models of contemporary style and boast a certain panache that is uniquely theirs. It is sometimes flashy but never sedate or—God forbid—mundane. The look, even when it is casual, appears to be completely pulled together and well thought out. While the rest of the world has happily embraced a casual lifestyle, Southerners have resisted, holding on firmly to stricter standards of style and grace. But it is this kind of stubborn reluctance that gives our culture an Old World elegance that others wish had never been so casually discarded by the rest of society.

We are not a breed of women who believe that our long locks should be shorn in a bowl-style cut immediately upon the arrival of our thirtieth birthday. I do worry sometimes, however, about my sister, who occasionally shows frightening tendencies toward that inclination. She is always well coifed, perfectly manicured, and beautifully attired, but she does have a couple of curiously odd ideas which are, I believe, reason for grave concern. She is never quite pleased with the length of my hair or of my skirts.

"You are too old to wear your hair that long and your skirts that short," she lectures, letting the eleven-year age difference between us show its mature face. She perturbs me or rather perplexes me, so I ignore her. Actually, I understand why she does it—she's in training to take mother's place when the time comes for our family matriarch to retreat to her heavenly reward where short skirts and long hair no longer matter. In fact, I bet the subject never even comes up in that celestial abode. I should add here that my sister is doing a darn fine job, too, as a matriarch-in-training. My beloved mother should be able to rest in sweet peace one day, knowing that her earthly shoes have been well filled.

But aside from my sister, Southern women have brazenly broken the rules of matronly womanhood. We no longer accept the staid disciplines of generations past. I often proudly marvel at my close friends from the frivolous days of long ago who have traveled the same stony path of time to a point that will, before we know it, be the center point that divides the fantasies of youth from the realities of maturity. Karen, Bridget, and Lisa, the same girls with whom I shared giggles of gossip and secrets of a teenage heart, are all more beautiful today than at that time so long ago that now lingers sweetly as happy, albeit blurred, memories. I believe, as my mother warned, we do care more today about how we look than we did as bright-eyed sixteen-year-olds. We all fret over the addition of a couple of pounds, work out routinely, exchange trendy makeup tips, and endlessly debate the merits of the latest hairstyles and fashions.

We Southern women put a lot of effort into how we look. With that in mind, we take a lot of pride (there's that sinful word again) in our appearance for our mate's sake as well as ours. My Aunt Linda, now in her fifties, is stunningly gorgeous with a perfect porcelain complexion and lovely strawberry blond hair. Over the years, she has carefully maintained her slender figure, accented by long legs. Not long ago, she gained five pounds after a decadent vacation that included several days of delicious key lime pie and delectable, fresh seafood. One day, she examined the weight gain in the mirror and fretfully asked my Uncle Jay, "Honey, if I get big and fat, will you still love me?"

"Yes, honey," he replied with an unflinching deadpan expression. "But I sure will miss you!"

We women of the South care deeply about how the men in our lives feel, and we expect them to return that courtesy and care deeply about how we feel. We take care of our looks for them and we expect that same kind of consideration from them. My uncle could get away with such an irreverent remark since his weight has not changed since their wedding day over thirty years ago. Southern men love well-dressed, well-coifed, well-maintained women. They appreciate the effort we put into looking good because we have *trained* them to be appreciative. Because of this appreciation, we are encouraged to keep up the rigorous work.

I was having lunch with three or four male colleagues when the conversation turned to women who work hard on their appearance.

"The older I get, the more work it takes," I grumbled. "It's getting to the point where it takes most of my time just to look halfway as good as I did ten years ago."

Until the day I die, I shall never forget the look of earnest sincerity that covered Mike's face, who was sitting directly across from me. "But let me tell you something," he said plaintively as he leaned across the table. "We men *appreciate* it when you women work hard to take care of yourselves."

The comment was so deeply heartfelt and adamant that everyone burst into a gurgling bubble of laughter. Still, Mike had made his point, and there are many times when I am trudging through one more mile on the treadmill that his words ring in my ears and give me that one push of encouragement I need. Men *do* appreciate it.

It's important to view the way you look as a marketing package that *sells* you to others. Companies put a lot of money and time into designing attractive, eye-catching packages so that consumers are drawn to those products on the shelves. We Southern women view ourselves as an overall marketing package that attracts people—particularly men—to us, personally and professionally. We know that looks do count because they say a lot about us before people have the opportunity to know us. Attractive packaging done either with pizzazz and color or quiet sophistication will lure more people to you and make them want to know you better.

Southern women work hard at trying to outdo one another. This one wants to be thinner than that one, that one wants a prettier dress than the one over there, and the one over there wants whiter teeth than the one over here. On and on it goes, but just like the Civil War, it is one of the best things to happen to the women of the South. This kind of healthy competition inspires us to be better, plus it enables us to create and maintain the vibrance that enlivens and emboldens our culture. No one ever took the time to write down the guidelines, but here are the previously unwritten rules:

We don't wear curlers or yard clothes to the grocery store. We do wear lipstick and mascara. Always. A trendy New Yorker asked me in wonderment, "Are you serious? Do you mean you *never* go to the store without lipstick and mascara?" I assured her that was indeed a fact, and she shook her head in *amazement*. When I reported back to my Southern sorority sisters the question I had been asked, each woman shook her head in *dismay*. "You mean they *don't?* In *New York?* You're kidding, right?" It's a difference in attitudes and priorities that does not mean that one is right and the other is not. This diversity is what makes America a wonderful, interesting place. But I will say that it only takes forty-four seconds to apply mascara and lipstick—fifty-three seconds if you add lip liner. And, personally, the way it improves my self-esteem is well worth a minute's worth of work.

We love bright colors and always find our most complimentary shades. Southerners have an obsession with color and, frankly, we're hard-pressed to understand New York's fascination with black. Southern women will always have one solid black outfit for a funeral, but for the two days prior to the funeral, more than likely, they'll wear black trimmed in leopard print or color. You will never find a lot of solid black in a Southern woman's closet. Women who are overweight often distract from their weight problem by wearing bold, bright-colored flowing outfits.

Shoes always match or complement our outfits. You will never see Southern women wearing black shoes with a beige outfit. And, they will never carry a navy purse with brown shoes. We'd prefer to go shoeless or purseless!

Southern ladies rarely go braless. We love the femininity of lingerie, and a true Southern woman considers it "trashy" not to wear a bra or hoisery (except on really hot summer days or when you want to feel exceptionally sexy, so bras and hose are tossed to the wind). A few women are so devoted, they even wear bras to bed!

Hairstyles and makeup are updated regularly—at least every twelve to eighteen months. It is important to change with the styles, or else you'll end up with something akin to a beehive hairdo. We would not be caught dead wearing bright blue eye shadow years after it is out of style.

Jeans are worn occasionally, not regularly. Southern women are still a little more formal than women in other areas of the country. Part of being the perfect lady means making an effort with your wardrobe and overall appearance. Sure, jeans and sweats are easy to throw on, and that's how they look—thrown together. There are still many proper Southern women who absolutely refuse to wear jeans at all.

Hats are back! Across the country, women are wearing hats again, but in the South, they never left. We wear them for formal occasions—Easter, weddings, funerals—and casual events such as shopping trips, fall college football games, and lunch with the girls.

Being overweight does not give you an excuse to look sloppy. In the South, fried foods are the staple of our cuisine—fried chicken, fried okra, fried green tomatoes, fried squash, even fried cornbread, biscuits, and grits! We also regularly practice our baking skills. As a result, we all struggle constantly with our weight. However, Southern women are expert at finding styles that flatter and hide figure flaws. It is a sad fact that every woman cannot wear every style or follow every trend. Put the time and effort into finding what works for you and stick to those styles.

Know what to wear where. We always wear black to funerals and rarely to weddings unless the bride has okayed it beforehand because it fits into the theme of the wedding.

Well-bred Southern women do not wear slacks to a funeral or to the funeral home to pay their respects. It is considered to be in bad taste. In fact, a Southern woman chooses very carefully when to wear slacks because dresses and skirts are more feminine.

Maintenance is a must. Many women in the South spend an admirable amount of time working to erase the heartless indignities created by the passage of years. We hit the pectoral machine at the gym in a valiant effort to coax sagging breasts back from the vicinity of the navel where they have thoughtlessly retreated. We buy bottles of hair color in vibrant shades and claim it is to add highlights, not cover gray. We suffer painful injections of salinelike solutions to erase those horrible spreading blotches of spider veins. We have varicose veins plucked from their gross cavernous abode in order to return our legs to their youthful clarity. And, when the time comes, a nip here and tuck there are completely acceptable.

I first met Dr. Richwine, our family plastic surgeon, when I was in college and he was fresh out of medical school with a scalpel so new it still had the price tag on it. My sister had suffered a horrible, disfiguring accident. Her baby had grabbed a much-too-large gold hoop in her pierced ear and given it a hard jerk. The resulting tear was not a pretty sight. The family fretted that she was scarred for life.

So, she made an appointment with the new, and albeit *only*, plastic surgeon in town and dragged me along. I was there to clutch firmly in my arms, the villainous child who had wrought such horrible damage upon his mother's beauty. Richwine stitched up the earlobe, later repierced it, and took great pride in his first such procedure. My sister, for her part, was returned to a certain normality for which the family was enormously grateful.

Now, years later, Richwine and I are buddies. We've been through spider vein injections, dog bites, medical facials, chemical peels, mole extractions, just to name a few. And, yes, I am afraid that sometimes I do treat his office as more of a beauty salon than a place of medical importance. Shallow, I know, but at least I admit it, and that goes a long way toward diluting the sins of my vanity.

Over the years, his practice has grown sufficiently so that he no longer depends on fifty-dollar earlobe jobs to pay the bills. When I stopped by his office to make an appointment one day, I looked up to see him sauntering down the hall in one of those green getups that look like the apparel of a college student rather than a man of some medical significance.

"Hi, Richwine," I called cheerfully, ignoring the long string of sacred alphabet letters that trail ceremoniously behind his name.

"What are you doing here?" he asked dryly. It's always nice to be welcomed so warmly. He was assisting a patient, a car accident victim who was covered with bruises, stitches, and casts. I was impressed with the doctor's compassion. I was particularly moved when he assisted the patient in using his crushed, mangled fingers to dig his billfold out of his pocket for payment.

"Making an appointment," I replied.

Then, did he ask for what? No. He immediately assumed that it was for something frivolous, unnecessary, and non–life threatening.

"Will you *please* get out of here and let me take care of

people who really need me!?!" He gestured wildly with those terrifically exaggerated expressions of his during which his face contorts comically, his eyes bulge, and his arms sweep the entire space around him.

"I beg your pardon?" I arched a warning eyebrow and threw an indignant hand on my hip.

"Come on. Get out of here. You don't need me."

"Well, isn't that a fine note?" I began a diatribe in the best imitation of my mother that I could muster. And I should add that after years of carefully observing her, I have become quite good at it, too. "May I remind you that it was *I* who cared when few others did? I, who have been your most devoted and most loyal patient? And now that your waiting room runneth over with big-ticket items, am I to be relegated to a list of unimportance and cast callously aside, never to be needed or wanted again? Have I now completely served my meager purpose in your life?"

He hung his head in shame, appropriately repentant and humbly asked, "When would you like an appointment?"

"That's more like it."

Then, I turned to Karen, his receptionist, and made my appointment for a facial.

CHAPTER SEVEN

The Artistry Behind a Southerner's Flirtatious Ways

For Southerners, flirtation is merely a descriptive word for being *reeeaaallll* nice. We flirt with everyone including other women, children, elderly folks, and, of course, or perhaps I should say *especially*, men. Our special brand of flirtation is not sexual, but rather a unique and useful people skill.

And, it is extremely effective.

There are two types of flirting—seductive and social. Any woman worth her weight in lip gloss knows how to flirt seductively, but the art of social flirting was born and perfected in the South. It comes as naturally to Southern women as the air we breathe, providing a pulsating heartbeat to our personal charisma. But any woman, with practice, can learn the art of this social skill and enjoy the benefits in personal, professional, and social relationships.

Women of the South are renowned for the art of social flirting. It is our trademark, much admired by many but occasionally scoffed at by others. Hollywood, in typical Tinsel Town fashion, sometimes caricatures the Southern woman's flirting skills. "Why, Horace, aren't you just the cleverest man who ever did walk on God's green earth!" the Southern belle in a bad B movie coos while the other women roll their eyes heavenward and Horace melts to a puddle at her feet. "I do declare! I just never have seen the likes of such cleverness in all my born days!"

Well, Hollywood got one part right—men do melt—but we are much more subtle and coy than that. Yes, we flutter, sparkle, tantalize, and titillate but we do so with feminine dignity and undeniable grace. And, occasionally, we even caricaturize ourselves by exaggerating our performance to the immense enjoyment and delight of other Southerners. We do what it takes to create as much levity as possible because laughter is the sustaining force behind life in the South.

We don't hesitate to laugh at ourselves (although we do not easily tolerate the mocking of non-Southerners). Good humor creates amicable situations, and those friendly situations develop into happy relationships. To some, social flirting may seem frivolous. It is not. It is essential. Why? Because it creates goodwill, makes others feel good (a most thoughtful, selfless thing to do!), and helps us get what we want.

We Southern women, like most women, are willful, but unlike other women, we are demure in our demands. We know how to get what we want, and we always get what we want unless we decide we don't want it anymore. We have tunnel vision that leads us to see only the desired end results, not the obstacles and detours that lie ahead. Problems are taken care of one by one when encountered.

Social flirting, of course, is a major tactic in our strategy.

But, most important, social flirting requires no heavy-handed hammering—a tactic that produces stress, resentment, ill will, anxiety, and, to top it off, is much less successful. Southern women know that happy, productive lives require the least amount of stress possible. Always conscious of reducing stress, we concentrate on making all situations win-win—winning at a high cost to others is not acceptable—by employing charm, thoughtfulness, and the coveted, sacred art of social flirting. We want everyone to be as happy as possible, especially ourselves.

The most important elements to social flirting that should never be forgotten are ingenuity and earnestness. There is no reason to spew forth insincere compliments or comments. There is *always* something good that can be said about every person and every situation. My grandmother always said, "If you can't say something good about someone, don't say anything at all." Of course, it was always amusing when minutes later, she shook her head disapprovingly and commented, "I know I shouldn't say this about Ethel, but she is the laziest woman I ever saw. She's so lazy, I don't see how she has the energy to breathe."

"But *you said* . . . ," one smart-mouthed grandchild would pipe up irreverently.

"Never you mind what I said," she would say, waving a dismissive hand. "A rose is a rose, a thorn is a thorn. And, that's all there is to it."

So, we're not perfect, but our intentions are good and frequently as pure as an early autumn frost. We are, however, utterly appalled at the rare Southern woman who engages in mindless chatter, producing a constant stream of babbling nonsense and false flattery. True Southern women will ostracize this kind of pretender from their inner circle and relegate her to the back pew of Southern society. Such women are the ones who *always* crave joining the Junior League but are blackballed. (Of course, they pretend that they wouldn't join even if the entire membership got down on their hands and knees and pleaded for their membership until the dew no longer falls on Dixie.)

Needless to say, this kind of woman is neither effective nor successful. She is a deplorable version of Southern womanhood. Sadly, we have our misfits. Gladly, they are few and far between.

Now that we have clawed viciously at the prickly rash that irritates the skin of our society, let's move toward the more useful instruction of proper social flirting. The key elements are:

A bright, sparkling smile
Soul-searching eyes
True sincerity
Inquisitiveness
A large database of general knowledge and useful information
Adulation for the other person expressed through flattery
A personal touch

A smile that comes from deep within and adds a lively sparkle to the eyes is an absolute must. It creates a happy countenance and makes a woman approachable, inviting, and nonthreatening. People are drawn to others who sparkle because a simple smile can cause the grim feelings of others to catapult upward. Good humor is the best and most effective stimulant in the world. It will put a captivatingly happy spin on interactions with others. Make a conscious effort to eliminate that slight scowl or pensive look, because the look on your face serves as an open invitation or a closed do-not-enter-at-all-costs door. A warm openness is key to the irresistible charm of Southern women.

If smiling doesn't come naturally, it can be developed through mind over matter. Think happy, heart-lifting thoughts. Focus on smiling and relieving facial tension that creates those grim, uninviting lines around the eyes and mouth. Be conscious of smiling and bringing the beauty that lies in your soul into your face.

Many accounts reveal that Shirley Temple's mother would remind her to "Sparkle, Shirley. Sparkle!" just before the cameras began to roll. Onlookers admitted that Shirley's transformation was dramatic. I've adapted this method myself, and I can tell you from personal experience that it does work. I, like many Southern women, use this technique when I'm attending a social function and I realize that I am distracted or tired. I take a deep breath as I enter a room, put on a big smile, and whisper to myself, "Sparkle! Sparkle!" Immediately, I feel my spirits lift and my face brighten.

To illustrate that sparkling truly works, I sometimes amuse myself by trying it in the busy hustle and bustle of airports, the very places where people are often too self-absorbed to notice others around them. I stumbled upon this terrific discovery by accident one day when I was distracted by the two miles I had to hike through the airport terminal wearing capriciously high heels while lugging a laptop computer and tugging the two tons of weight that I fondly refer to as my carry-on luggage. Suddenly, I became aware of the furrow between my brows and my unattractive grimace. Too many times we are not aware of our facial expressions because our minds are so busy with other things.

On that particular day in the airport, when I realized what a grim, unfriendly look I wore, I also noticed something else. No one was paying any attention to me. Like most Southern women, I do not like to be unnoticed. We create attention-getting personas because a significant amount of attention is vital to our health. To our very survival. Actually, all women—especially Southern ones—crave attention and when we do not get it, marriages fail, job performances decline, and self-esteem droops. Southern women on the whole are happier because we know how to siphon from others every little drop of attention possible. Therefore, we feel nurtured and appreciated.

Back to the airport. No one was noticing me. And I mean no one. You know the kind of acknowledgment you normally get from strangers—a brief nod, a slight smile, a fleeting glance. Not me. I was getting nothing. *Nada.* Zilch.

So, I decided to sparkle. I lowered my chin and brought forth the transformation from deep within. I loosened the muscles in my forehead so that the furrow disappeared as well as those disdainful lines that continue to carve themselves deeper into my forehead as the years pass. I relaxed my entire face, blinked my eyes several times to illuminate my eyes with a dewy twinkle, and wet my lips for a glimmering shine. "Sparkle, sparkle," I whispered to myself as I raised my head again. The new me greeted the airport patrons with a radiant smile that I pasted solidly on my face.

The reaction was immediate and amazing. Men and women reacted to my bubbly allure with friendly smiles, nods, and even greetings of "hello." From the corner of my eye, I noticed that people waiting at the gates put down their newspapers or halted conversation to watch me trudge by. I still looked the same, wore the same clothes as moments before, but the difference was a seductive sparkle from my eyes, an enticing smile, and an overall glowing facial expression. I no longer carried a sign across my face that blared "Stay out! Leave me alone! I have a lot on my mind and no time for you!" My expression now said, "Hello! How are you? Hope you're having a great day!" People who were disgruntled with delayed flights, missed appointments, and other problems responded positively to my joyous look.

I had done the nearly impossible in a busy, international airport. I stood out in the crowd! The Southern belle heart in me beat rapidly with joy at the accomplishment and the attention it had wrought. If something like that can take place in a run-you-over, knock-you-down airport, imagine what can happen when you enter the room for a cocktail party or small dinner gathering? Or better yet, for an intimate one-on-one with that very special someone. It works. Try it and see.

Next to a brilliant smile, the most important element of successful social flirting is the appealing use of the eyes. They are truly the windows to our souls. I know a man who will look you directly in the eyes in an effort to be sincere, but his eyes are vacuous, completely devoid of expression or emotion. He looks like a robot. I honestly have never seen anyone else who did not have any depth—even a modicum—of feeling revealed in the eyes. Then, one day it occurred to me. He has no soul! For surely, if he had a soul that felt emotion of any kind, his eyes would betray that it lies deeply buried within. Mechanically, he always says and does the right thing—those things that are expected in the appropriate circumstances. But his lack of sincerity isolates him from others who are obviously uncomfortable with his robotic gestures. It dramatically diminishes the effectiveness of an otherwise smart, polished individual.

Eyes are very important for every look from a soul-searching direct gaze to a fluttery, flirtatious glance. Use them for all they're worth. Southern women excel at this. Flirtatiously, we use our eyes in a coy manner. We lower our heads slightly, slyly toss a sideward glance combined with a small, tight smile. Then the head is raised slowly as we look up—still with the head turned to the side, not facing the other person—through mascara-tinged lashes. The late Princess Diana was extraordinarily good at this look, and it was extremely effective. Visualize all those photos of her with a tight-lipped smile, looking up shyly with the glance directed to the side, and you have the perfect picture of this efficacious use of the eyes. The world's masses adored this enchanting look, but it was nothing new to the women of the South. We have employed this technique since the early days of Southern civilization.

At other times, we use our eyes to draw people to us from across the room or from two feet away. It's easy to do. Make direct eye contact (again with the sparkle), tilt your head forward slightly toward the object of your attention, and smile with confidence (a no-teeth-showing look works best here). Then slowly pull your head back. Subconsciously and subtly, you have drawn that person closer to you and created a stronger, intimate bond. It's the same effect we create when we nuzzle our cheek against a lover or lean closely to the ear of a friend to share a secret. Doing so welcomes people into your extremely intimate circle of private space.

When you really want to score points, look deeply into

someone's eyes and hang on for dear life to every word that drips from his or her lips. This is more easily done in an intimate setting than in a large gathering, so it takes discipline and concentration. I personally hate to talk to someone whose eyes are constantly flitting around the room who then nods and greets others. Without fail, they then have the nerve to say, "Go ahead, I'm listening to you." In contrast, perfect social flirting makes one person at a time feel like the most important one in the world to you. No one can resist that scrumptious feeling.

Those are the do's. Here is a big don't. A sweeping head-to-toes glance of someone is disconcerting, rude, and puts the other person ill at ease. That look says, "You're under inspection, and I'm not particularly impressed by what I see." To make someone feel valued and important, never look below the chin while in conversation. Of course, in the South, this kind of chastising look does have certain merit at times. We save it for those stupid, mindless chatterers whom we want to drive quickly from our presence. Complete rejection is accomplished easily by raising one eyebrow, coolly assessing their appearance from top to bottom, and icily saying, "Hello, how are you?" You'd be surprised at how quickly this drives those undesirables from our midst!

Sincerity is crucial, since this kind of flirting is not empty-headed. It takes a smart woman to flirt socially. Sincerity, not fluff and bluff, is the foundation of comments. Don't just say something because it sounds good rolling off your tongue. Say it because you mean it and because your saying it will mean a great deal to the other person. It is better to give a tiny compliment that is completely genuine than a huge one that is insincere. People know. Believe me, they know.

Inquisitiveness is essential to social flirting because it demonstrates that you are caring and thoughtful. Again, your questions have to be sincere and genuine or people will know you are bluffing. I have always found that a few minutes of conversation will introduce a subject of mutual interest that will lead to an enthusiastic discussion. To reach that point, ask deep, probing questions that display a genuine interest in the other person. Ask ones like "Where did you go to school?" "Where were you born?" "How do you know our hostess?" "How long have you been with the company?" "Have you seen that new movie that opened last week?" Within five questions, you will hit on something that sparks a lively dialogue and will lead the way to deeper discussion. It's important to avoid yes and no questions. If you ask a question that is answered with one word, rework it in a way that requires the person to expound further. Demonstrate further interest through facial expressions that show wonderment, awe, interest, sympathy, understanding, and empathy to what the other person is saying. Southern women respond warmly and graciously to the words of others. Two minutes of warmth wins more friends than two years of cool detachment.

Seduction, be it social or sexual, comes from the mind. Any woman can flash skin, but the most irresistible damsel is the one who seduces and flirts with a sharp, knowledgeable mind.

Part of the Southern woman's charm is derived from her ability to be a good conversationalist who has a wide range of knowledge. She never closes her mind to new information and strives to know a little bit about everything. Those tiny seeds of knowledge enable her to converse with anyone on a variety of subjects. Knowing a little bit about everything requires some time and dedication, but it is, without a doubt, the most effective, impressive skill you can cultivate.

I subscribe to sixteen different publications on such a wide range of topics that I am certain that my mail carrier is amused by my eclectic tastes. From news magazines to a financial newspaper to a World War II magazine to entertainment, fashion, business, society, I span a wide range. Friends often laugh at the diversity of titles found scattered on my coffee table. The ironclad rule in my household is that a magazine or newspaper is never thrown away unread. I surf the Internet daily for new info and insights. I read the top books on the best-seller lists, know which stocks are performing well and which aren't. As a result, I rarely, if ever, am incapable of contributing some tidbit, no matter how tiny, to a conversation. People, particularly men, are often amazed and frequently impressed.

Knowledge gives substance to your conversation, and substance gives you credibility. It is the most productive thing you can do to enhance your social flirting skills. A smart Southern woman never closes her mind to learning about new people, places, or things, and once she has that knowledge, she knows how to use it. You will find, without fail, that if you are not initially interested in a subject, once you take the time to learn a little bit about it, you will develop interest.

When I was a young sportswriter, my editor assigned me to cover a stock car race. I was appalled. Devastated. I haughtily informed him it was beneath me (after all, I was enrolled in an aristocratic women's college where steeplechases were accepted forms of entertainment—stock car races were not). When that didn't work, I begged. Then I threatened to quit (he asked if I could give him two weeks' notice). I told him I didn't know anything about car races. He said I could learn. And I did.

Although I hated the first few races, the participants and fans were so enthusiastic and friendly, I began to warm to it. The drivers and crew chiefs eagerly and patiently explained the rules and mechanics of the sport. Within two months, I was completely hooked. I didn't like the sport when I had no *knowledge* or understanding of it. Once I had knowledge, I had interest. Then, there was no stopping me. I am so grateful to that mean ole editor who insisted on that assignment because many of my dearest friendships are a result of the people I met in motor sports. Had I chosen to remain ignorant about racing, I would have cheated myself out of many wonderful blessings and experiences.

Social flirting screams for an ample amount of flattery. Southern women are well-trained flatterers because they are tenacious observers (some might say scrutinizers). We notice the tiniest details, and that kind of attention means a lot to people.

Again, here's the key to compliments—you have to *mean* them! People instinctively know the sincerity or insincerity of a compliment and to many, insincerity is a serious form of mockery. Southern women believe there is good in everyone. We quickly find that good and comment on it. Positive comments are particularly important when first meeting someone because they get everything off to a good start. They are helpful in tearing down those primal protective, mental fences that keep relationships from flourishing and being totally successful. We believe in moving quickly to charmingly disarm before the holes are even dug for those fence posts.

The final component to social flirting is the ever-important personal touch. Southerners are great touchers and huggers, which to us are coveted gestures of warmth. Other regions, however, are naturally more standoffish and do not like the invasion of personal space. However, a very slight touch of the fingertip against an arm or a hand on occasion adds a slight intimacy and important bonding to any encounter.

We hug with gusto by grabbing the recipient in a full body lock. Then, if we really like the person, when we stop hugging, we hand-squeeze for a couple of minutes as we flirtatiously flatter with sparkling smiles and deep eye contact. Instead of a hand squeeze, a not-quite-so-good friend receives an arm slung loosely around her shoulders after the big hug or an arm playfully tucked cozily through his. Other times, the hug is followed by a touch on the arm or nothing at all. Even in the business world, we stretch the rules (yes, many Southern women do not hesitate to hug business colleagues—not the ones they see on a daily basis but the ones they see every *other* day). It is not unusual for a Southern woman to shake hands with a gentleman or another woman and then create additional intimacy by placing her other hand on top of the handshake and stepping closer toward the other person. It is our way of adding warmth to a cold business world.

One day, I bumped into an old acquaintance of mine. Kelly was standing in front of me at the grocery checkout when she turned slightly toward me and said hello with cool detachment. Now, let me explain something right here before I go further with this sad tale. Kelly was one of the most beautiful, enchanting Southern belles you could ever have hoped to meet. Men and women alike marveled at her unparalleled beauty, grace, and charm. Then, she moved north to Detroit for several years and, quite frankly, it just about ruined her.

Apparently much of her Southern warmth got frozen in those merciless winters. So, to make a long story short, no one is allowed to hug or overtly touch Kelly anymore. In deference to her acquired preference, I reached out and touched her forearm ever so lightly with a fingertip and said "Hello, Kelly! How are you?" I told you—a true Southerner has to touch just as we have to devour fried foods. It's an obsessive habit. Fortunately, it was an appropriate compromise that suited us both and still added the intimacy I wished to convey to an old friend.

Smart Southern women always follow instinct rather than impulse. We spot quickly those who adore a hug, those who detest it, and those who need it. Then, we deftly adjust the social flirting approach to the level of comfort desired by the other person. That is why social flirting is an art, a skill carefully crafted by generations who diligently studied the tiniest details and honed the skill to perfection.

Certainly, it takes practice, but those women who retreat hastily from attempting full-hearted flirting will never taste the sweet nectar of success that resides permanently on the tongue of the polished, prominent social flirter.

CHAPTER EIGHT

When We Want to Overpay, We Shop at Neiman Marcus

Now, don't get me wrong. Neiman Marcus is a fabulous store: the epitome of high class lovingly purchased with a lot of cash. But those folks at the swankiest department store that the South ever gave birth to just don't understand the meaning of the word *bargain*. Or, for that matter, the word *negotiation*.

If you doubt my words of unflinching honesty bought with hard-earned experience, then just sashay yourself through those famous doors and try to talk the haughty saleslady down on the price of a Chanel purse. Won't happen. I can promise you. Don't even try to use one of those 10 percent discount cards you get for opening a charge account. She'll sniff pretentiously and look at you as though you are cashing in your last food stamps. Just plop down the money for the asking price plus tax. Class costs money. And sometimes, I have discovered, it costs more than I can afford.

That's why I learned the priceless art of negotiation.

The ability to negotiate is a great skill to possess. For some reason, many women consider negotiation to be unladylike, but in the South we don't. We just do it in a ladylike manner.

When Southern women pull out all the stops in a negotiation, they are undeniably unbeatable. That combination of shrewdness, intelligence, and fluttery charm is lethal to the other party. We drown the unsuspecting seller in dripping sweetness and femininity, throwing a life jacket at the last moment in the form of a cashier's check. The single, greatest mistake a woman can make in negotiation is to lose her femininity and deal like a man. When she loses that, she loses her winning, profitable edge—against men or women.

By the way, don't allow those insidious thoughts of discrimination to float through the river of your mind, those thoughts that nudge you and whisper, "This will only work when you negotiate against men." Absolutely not. Women like to be flattered and charmed, too. Even by other women.

The bottom line to a successful negotiation is that everyone wins, but you win more. You purchase something at a more reasonable price while the seller unloads the item at less profit but frees up restrained capital. Always remember that regardless of the price you settle on, you have done the buyer or seller a favor, for whatever reason. If she didn't want or need to buy or sell, she wouldn't agree to the price.

I have a girlfriend who has developed this art of enchanting feminine negotiation into a fine science. Karen is the only person I know who can buy a new BMW for the price of an old Volkswagen! She charms, flirts, and bats her mascara-coated eyelashes until the seller becomes rattled. Then, she uses her razor-sharp business mind to cut the final deal.

It is disgusting. Absolutely nauseating. Such a blatant misuse of the precious, cherished gift that God gave only to us women! But Karen promises to keep working with me until I get it absolutely perfect. I'm almost there.

I got my first remarkable deal through utterly brilliant (it's my book so I get to pick the adverbs and adjectives) negotiation several years ago. Now, let me tell you about it. Once you negotiate a bargain that puts others in awe of your business acumen, there's no stopping the restless beast that demands a bargain. It's like a Carolina moonshiner outrunning the law on a clear, starry night. There will be no catching you.

The more that people rave about your cleverness, the more the beast will struggle to break free of its once limited confines, reaching out its deadly claws to grab its next victim and choke out a bargain that's too good to believe.

It happened to me. And suddenly I was possessed of an insatiable desire to one-up everyone and claim a bargain. It was almost to the point where I thought of seeking help from Negotiators Anonymous. Thank goodness, that proved to be unnecessary.

I was in the market for a new car, the old one having ingeniously caught fire and burned to the enjoyment of a vast crowd at a shopping mall. Even before my old car (and I would just like to tell Detroit at this point that I don't consider four years "old" for a car either) chose immolation as a form of escaping my grasp, I had been shopping for another one. I was a publicist on NASCAR's Winston Cup Series and that year, one of my drivers won the prestigious Daytona 500. Speedway officials drove the winner and me from the winner's circle to the press box for postrace interviews.

I crawled into the most beautiful sports car that I have ever seen. To this day, I have not seen one snazzier. It looked like a rocket ship on the inside with a digital dashboard and sounded like one when the guy hit the accelerator.

"This is me!" I announced to the passengers. "I must have a car like this."

I returned from Daytona and began to search dealerships for this hot, must-have-at-any-cost car. Each dealer shook his head in bewilderment, claiming to know of no such animal. They showed me analog versions of the same car and tried to persuade me by intimating that I had only dreamed up this car. By the way, that infuriated me. I hate having my limited intelligence insulted.

A few months later, when I was in immediate need of a car after the burnout, I returned to a previously visited dealership. The salesman ran out, waving his arms and jabbering excitedly.

"I can't believe you're here! We got in a car yesterday exactly like what you were looking for." Saliva was beginning to bubble from the edge of his mouth. Salespeople get that way when they feel a sure commission coming on. "We found out that they only made a limited number of these. This one belonged to an executive of the car manufacturer. It only has thirty-five hundred miles on it."

I was excited, too. But I knew enough to swallow my saliva rather than let the greedy salesman see it. When he showed me the car, I almost choked on my saliva. It was everything I was looking for. Perfect. Even the color was exactly what I wanted: white with tan interior and fancy gold wheels.

I took it for a test drive and I knew I had to have that car.

"How much?" I asked as I crawled out of the spaceship. (I would also like to pause here and tell the gods of sports cars that it is very difficult to be a lady and disembark from one of those low-slung designs. And don't even try it in a short skirt if you have an aversion to showing anything your mother told you not to show.)

"Well, it has a full package of options on it. New, it listed for twenty-five thousand, but since it's a used executive car—and should I remind you what extraordinary care they take of their cars? Treat them like babies."

"The price?"

"Oh yes. We're firm at twenty-one seven."

That was a lot of money for a car back in those years (I'm beginning to sound like my grandmother, God forbid). But I wanted that car, and it was worth every penny to me. Yet, I didn't bite although I was beginning to dew puddles through my silk blouse. (In the South, women "dew"; we never perspire.) I was afraid—no, make that terrified—that someone else would snatch the car away before I could buy it.

"Let me think about it. I'll come back this afternoon."

At this point, I would like to say that I was clever enough to play a savvy game of cat-and-mouse with him. You know, held my cards close to my chest so he couldn't see the lousy hand I was playing. I would like to say that I was cool enough and smart enough to walk off that car lot, knowing the salesman would pant hungrily after me and be willing to cut a better deal when I returned.

I would like to say I was that smart. But I wasn't. It was plain, good, old-fashioned Southern manners that pulled me reluctantly from the spiritual bonding I had discovered with that beautiful sports car.

I left out of loyalty to someone who had been very good to me and whose goodness I couldn't easily dismiss. Southerners tend to be a fairly loyal bunch, and we pretty much believe in "dancing with the one what brung you to the dance." So, I drove to another dealership up the street where I had purchased two previous cars and where the general manager had always gone above and beyond the call of good customer service. He was fair, honest, and always looked out for me when there was a problem. Come to think about it, I wonder now where he was when that other car caught on fire.

"Wayne, I need to talk to you." I was a little nervous.

He threw a thumb toward the direction of his office. "C'-mon in."

I explained that I had finally found the exact car I was looking for, but it was at another dealership. Wayne knew how difficult the car had been to find because he and his staff had exhausted every possible effort to locate a similar vehicle.

"Good!" he exclaimed enthusiastically. "I'm glad. Have you bought it, yet?"

I shook my head. "I wouldn't do that without discussing it with you first."

"Me?" He looked puzzled.

"That's right. You've been awfully good to me and I greatly appreciate it. Will it be a problem with you if I buy a car from another dealership?"

He smiled, then shook his head vigorously. "Not at all. I can't get that car for you, so go buy it where you can."

I guess it's true that good follows good and bad follows bad because before I left, Wayne rewarded my consideration with my first major lesson in negotiation. And if you must know, it was he, Dr. Frankenstein, Jr., who created the negotiation monster I became.

"How much are you going to offer for that car?" he asked as I started to get up from the chair.

I shrugged. "Oh, I don't know. Maybe twenty-one thousand. What do you think?"

He leaned back in his desk chair and looked me squarely in the eyes, and had it not been for that square look, I would have thought he was joking. "Offer him thirteen five."

"What!" I screeched, falling back down into the chair. "Have you lost your mind! He'll laugh me out of that dealership."

He smiled smugly. It's that smile that still haunts me today when I go car shopping. Those car people know a whole lot more than they're telling.

"So?" he asked. "What have you got to lose?"

"Are you serious? That's seventy-five hundred lower than asking. That's ridiculous." As soon as I had calculated the savings in my feeble brain, I asked anxiously, "Do you think he'd take it?"

"It's worth a try. You can negotiate up from there."

I was still unsure when I left the dealership, and had I not implicitly trusted Wayne, I would never have attempted such a harrowing feat. But I did trust him and I gave it a whirl.

"I'm ready to make an offer," I announced when I returned to the other dealership. He began to drool.

"Come in my office," he said between deep gasps for breath.

I sat down and folded my hands in my lap. "I'll give you thirteen five for the car."

My earlier reaction to Wayne's suggestion was nothing compared to his. He started to hyperventilate and immediately I wanted to cry out, "Please don't die! I'll give you what you're asking."

But I restrained myself, and then a full-fledged negotiation began. When it ended a couple of hours later, I had bought my dream car for fourteen seven and gotten a lot of extras thrown in like gas and increased warranty. I did not, however, get the radar detector I asked for. I'm still miffed about that.

What a lesson I learned that day! A lesson that has saved me so much money since then and enabled me to buy things I could not have afforded otherwise. You never know how much less someone is willing to take, unless you ask. So, don't be afraid to ask.

Strangely enough, women are born negotiators, but most do not even realize it. In fact, at the art of negotiation, women are often better than men. The difference is that women aren't as comfortable carrying it to the ragged edge as men. Therefore, women will often back down before getting the best deal possible. Men, on the other hand, will hammer it out until the last dollar is discounted.

But women, who use disarming charm, can get a much better deal than any man could ever dare to. Don't be afraid or reluctant to use your feminine wiles to get a great deal. Those luscious wiles are part of the survival skills we're given at birth. God expects us to use them. I'm sure He does.

A few months after negotiating that awesome deal, I saw the sales guy at the grocery store. Notice that I didn't say, "ran into him at the grocery store"? That's because he ran away from me. You know how people see you but pretend not to see you and then dodge you by going down another aisle? I didn't let him get away that easily because, quite frankly, I liked him. I've noticed you tend to like people better than they like you when you're the one who prevails in a deal.

"I love my car!" I gushed.

"Good. Good," he said in a polite but terse tone. "You got

an unbelievable bargain. I keep getting reminded of that at the dealership."

"Well, I appreciate it," I replied cheerfully. "I really enjoyed doing business with you."

"I bet you did," he mumbled, picking up a carton of ice cream. He started to walk off, then stopped and turned back around. "Hey, will you do me a favor?"

"Sure."

"Next time you need a car, there's a guy I'd like for you to go and see." He gave me the name of the salesman and the other dealership at which he worked. "I'd consider it a personal favor if you'd look at buying a car from him."

I nodded slowly as a look of wise understanding slowly crept across my face. "You don't like him, do you?"

"Hate him. Absolutely hate him," he admitted before disappearing from my life forever.

Since that valuable lesson, I have bought a house, cars, computers, clothes, furniture, and various other things by incorporating what I learned. I have saved a small fortune.

I used to cringe with embarrassment when my oldest sister would bargain for an item. She never buys anything without negotiation, and she starts so absurdly low that even I am embarrassed. But she always saves money, and the bottom line is that money is too hard earned for anyone to just throw it away.

Through trial, error, and watching attentively the wondrous efforts of other Southern women, I have uncovered a few tricks that really do work.

Charm, flirt, and flatter ridiculously. If you must, revisit the chapter on social flirting and then lay it to 'em. Social flirting encourages a person to lower her guard and become more relaxed. Aren't you easier to get along with when you're in a good mood and not tensely cautious? When you're relaxed, aren't you more willing to go with the flow, wave your hand, and say breezily, "Whatever." That's the premise behind this negotiation tactic: Relax the seller and put him in a more willing frame of mind to accept a low offer.

Wear a short skirt. I do have to admit here that this is one negotiation tactic that appears to work better on men than on other women. However, it works so exceedingly well with men that it more than offsets the lack of influence it has on other women. It does, though, work beautifully with some women because the short skirt causes them to misjudge your ability. They think you're nothing more than a silly trollop, which is a wonderful thing for them to think. It's much easier to really zing the unsuspecting ones!

The rule of thumb is that the higher the skirt, the higher the discount. Remember that long skirts mean high prices, short skirts mean lower prices. If you don't like short skirts or think you don't look good in them, just show up in the most dazzling, flattering outfit you own.

Ask a lot of questions. Even stupid questions. *Especially* stupid questions. Doing so always makes them think that you don't know what you're doing. Let 'em think that. In fact, you want them to think that because there goes the old guard letting down again. Then, when they least expect it, hammer the deal home.

Do your research and homework. Know every detail about the item that you are purchasing. Use consumer guides, newspapers, magazines, and the Internet to know everything you need to know. If it is a big item like a house, car, or boat, the deal could take months. Do not skip this step because it will cost you money. Knowledge is the most powerful asset in negotiation, and the seller is hoping that you will have very little of it when you begin to negotiate.

Determine your maximum price and stick to it. After doing your research, review your bank account and decide how much you'll pay for the item. Stick to it. Never go higher, because you'll regret it later. This is where emotion comes in over the analytical process, and I can tell you that emotion will *always* pay more than analytical thought.

If you're looking for a bargain on a non-necessary item, don't be timid about really low-balling your offer. Janice saw an ad for a large ski boat that she didn't need, but one she had always wanted. Because she had always followed the cost of these boats, she knew the price was very fair. Still, she offered $5,000 less. The seller almost choked. "No way," he exploded. "I'm asking wholesale on it now."

She stood her ground. Although she wanted the boat, it wasn't a necessity. Three months later, the seller called and said if the offer still stood, he would take it. She bought the ski boat, used it for two years, and sold it at a profit for the price that the original seller had asked.

If you feel you're about to go higher than your predetermined price, stop yourself. Whatever it takes, stop yourself. Take a bathroom break or, better yet, stop for the day. Think it over during the evening and return the next day after your emotions have cooled.

Hold your cards close to your chest. Don't give up your power to the other party by sharing your knowledge—

especially when you're the seller. If someone knows you *have* to sell your house, the price just plummeted. A simple rule of economics: Demand drives price. On the other hand, if you know that the other person has to sell, don't divulge that you know. Don't get chatty and share too much. Personally, this is the biggest challenge for me. I got the propensity to talk too much from my mother.

Never state the first price. If you're negotiating to buy something and there is an advertised price, begin by saying "What's your best price?" They'll begin to hem and haw, but hear them out. The bargaining has begun.

If it's a job you're after, refuse to name your price first. Even if you have to throw yourself down on the floor and wail loudly, "But I don't wanna tell!" Like my cousin Emma Lou. It always works for her. You need to know what the company's willing to offer because it's possible that it's more than you're thinking of asking.

A friend of mine hired someone for a position that he had been trying to fill for several months. When an ideal candidate appeared, my friend asked, "What kind of salary do you expect?"

The candidate cleared his throat and said, "Well, I've studied your numbers and I believe you should be able to afford what I want." Then, proud of the sleuthing he had done, he named his salary.

My friend tried not to appear too anxious when he agreed to the salary. It was 30 percent lower than he had been willing to pay. What a mistake the new employee had made! Based on the average annual salary increase, it will take that guy years to get to the salary that he could have had from the beginning. That'll turn your milk sour.

Never fall in love. With men, yes. With possessions, no. If you fall in love with an item, you will always pay more. To get the best deal possible, it is crucial to stay emotionally detached. This, of course, is much harder for women than men since we are more sensitive and compassionate. But tell yourself, "If I don't get this car at the right price, I'll find a better car and better deal later." And, you will. Remember: Southern women preach and practice "patience."

Negotiate from a position of strength. Find your strength through various means such as bringing something special to the table (all cash, for instance) or knowing why the other person needs to sell (a divorce often means the house has to go) or why they're desperate to buy.

Trust your instincts. Women are very intuitive, so if you have a "bad" feeling about the seller or situation, walk away. If you instinctively feel that you're paying too much, pull out of the deal. You will never go wrong by listening to your woman's intuition.

Use all your people skills. Negotiation is a time to be firm and self-assured, not a time to be arrogant and condescending. *Remember to charmingly disarm.* If you are asking for a promotion or raise, be well prepared by listing your skills, dedication, accomplishments, and such. Make the pitch as to why you are ready for additional responsibility and advancement. Do not compare yourself with someone else by saying "I've been here six months longer than Mary Grace, and she was promoted last month." Corporations today rarely base raises and promotions on seniority alone but rather on skills, loyalty, and potential.

Then, if all else fails, use the top-secret weapon of all Southern women: Bake 'em a pie.

CHAPTER NINE

Accent Your Life with Laughter

(Even If It Isn't in a Southern Accent)

HUMOR IS NOT only important in the South; it is life sustaining. We take our humor seriously and practice it religiously. Have you ever heard anyone called a *Northern* humorist? I rest my case.

Southerners make a conscious effort to find humor in all situations and do not wallow in self-pity. Enthusiastic laughter is the best remedy for alleviating overwhelming stress and enjoying more productive, sane lives.

A couple of years ago, my dad was in the hospital, lying literally at death's door. A dark pall was hanging over the family and one night as we all gathered glumly in his room, he tried to lift the mood by asking about a close friend.

"He's doing just as he pleases like he always does," I replied dryly.

"Well, I don't blame him," my dad responded. "If I were worth twenty million, I'd do just as I please too."

"Daddy," I shot back quickly, "if you were worth twenty million, we wouldn't be trying so hard to keep you alive right now!"

When I saw the stunned looks on everyone's faces, immediately I wished that I could grab the words and stuff them back into my mouth. There were a couple of uncomfortable seconds when I wanted to drop through the floor and land in the insane ward where I belonged. However, my dad, the ringleader of humor in our family, began to laugh and was soon joined by everyone else. That laughter immediately lifted the heaviness in the room and revived our energy.

To the chagrin of a couple of nurses to whom he had been less than polite, Daddy *did not* die. When his condition had greatly improved, his irascibility returned and the nurses were the unfortunate recipients of his grouchiness. Finally, one of the more formidable nurses had had enough. She was almost out the door one day when she turned to him and asked, "Do you know *why* you didn't die?"

He looked at her suspiciously and growled under his breath.

"Because God *didn't want* you!" She turned quickly on her heel and retreated to our howls of laughter, including Daddy's.

A friend of mine suffered a traumatic head injury several years ago and after she recovered medically, the doctors decided to assign her to the hospital's psychiatric ward for a few days of tests before her release. This was a real treat for those of us who went to visit her on that special floor because we are not accustomed to seeing our beloved eccentrics clustered together in one big group. We're used to dealing with them on a one-on-one basis in everyday life.

While we were there, we noticed a frail woman who

looked to be in her mid-fifties wandering the halls, tightly clutching a big, black Bible to her chest as though it was her most precious possession. If someone came close to her, she would hover protectively over the Bible, hunching over it and drawing herself away from them. Then, she would mutter something and move on. After an hour or so, however, she got brave enough and ventured into the visiting room where we were gathered. She made the mistake of sitting close to my friend, who is the friendliest, kindest soul in the world and never meets a stranger she doesn't like.

My friend smiled brightly and sweetly. "Hello!" she exclaimed with a beaming smile, eager to make a new friend while the rest of us smiled and greeted the cautious apostle with what we thought was tremendous sweetness. "I notice that you carry your Bible with you all the time. I love my Bible, too. What's your favorite scripture?"

Panic filled the woman's eyes and she jumped up quickly from the sofa. Before she beat a quick retreat, she took in with a sweeping glance the offending creatures who had dared to speak to her. She lifted her head heavenward and announced in a strong, authoritative voice, "See there, Jesus! *I told you* there were crazy people in here!"

While Southerners laugh delightedly in the good times, we laugh determinedly at life's troubles. It is that humor that pulls us through when the tunnel is dark and the power company has turned off the light at the end of the tunnel. When you call the power company to complain and plead for light, you receive that recording that says "Our office is now closed. Please call back on Wednesday between twelve noon and twelve-fifteen P.M. for assistance. And, if we aren't out to lunch, we will be happy to speak with you."

Difficult times are when it is *most* important to laugh. Joking about a bad situation alleviates some of the gloom and makes any situation appear brighter. Spoken words can either be our most powerful ally or our enemy. The choice is ours. The mind believes what it hears and when we bemoan our problems, our minds, which guide our actions, operate on negative power. Southern women are eternally optimistic, and many times you will hear one explain, "Well, it could be worse." Then, she'll tell you *what* could be worse. More often than not, she'll add a comic remark or facial expression.

Look for humor in everything. It's there. Sometimes, it just requires a lot of digging.

My sister's mother-in-law unfortunately suffers from Alzheimer's. As anyone knows who has ever dealt with an Alzheimer's patient, it is extremely difficult and trying for all those involved. Yet, their family tries hard to seek comic relief from time to time to deal with the situation. Even the patient, a strong-willed, powerful woman, joins in by spouting off admonishments to others such as "Well, you know my mind's not good anymore, but even I know better than to do something like that!"

She is a tough woman. Although in her late seventies, she can throw a seventy-five-pound bale of hay as effortlessly as her athletic sons and grandsons. A former beauty queen at the age of sixteen, she is still a striking woman with a lot of pizzazz. In the initial stages of the disease, she was sent to a specialist who bored her senseless with his tireless questions as he put her through a mentally grueling test.

"Now, can you tell me who the governor is?" he asked after an hour of such questions.

She had finally had enough. "Of course I can," she retorted sharply, delivering the answer perfectly. Then, stubbornly she threw her shoulders back, leaned closer, and wagged her finger in his face. "And *don't* ask me who the president is, either," she warned in a severe tone. "That's what got me sent over here in the first place!"

Sometimes we have to laugh at ourselves because humor is the only thing that sustains us during the difficult times. There are times when we have to focus the joke on ourselves because it is important for others to laugh with us. I once worked in a corporation that was rocked by a gossipy scandal involving a top officer. As a result, the company faced a complete upheaval and was quickly sold. It was a difficult time for everyone in general, and for me in particular, because I had been drawn into the center of the gossip. The rumor around the water cooler was that the trouble stemmed from the embattled executive's leaving his devoted, highly regarded wife of thirty-plus years for a younger woman, presumably someone in the company. There were five or six names whispered around. However, guess who won the dubious starring role in the gossip mill? Yep, little ole me. I was devastated. Shunned and deserted by many, I saw nothing funny about the situation. It was torturous and hurtful. As director of corporate communications, I had to deal with the press and when the executive assured me that none of the gossip was true, I believed him and dutifully declared or rather preached his innocence to media across the nation. I *knew* it wasn't me, but that's all I personally knew as fact.

The tension created by the rumormongers was overwhelming. One day, a dear friend, also a member of the senior management team, stopped by my office to take me to lunch.

He has a terrific sense of humor and was bold enough to ask when we started to leave, "Do you think that people will think *we're* having an affair if we go to lunch together?"

His timing was perfect, because it was time to start laughing at the situation. I tilted my head to the side, put my hands on my hips, and looked at him as if he had lost his mind. "Are you crazy?" I asked. "Why would anyone think I'm running around with you? After all, they all think I've got something going with the big boss. *Why* on earth would I need *you?*"

We looked at each other for a moment and burst into laughter that lasted for several minutes. We couldn't stop laughing. That was the turning point for me. We both repeated the story throughout the company, and I made other such jokes. It was so disarming that people began to laugh with me, rather than talking about me behind my back. This much improved attitude got me through the remainder of a difficult period.

As for the executive, he ended up marrying a woman in the company who would have been hard-pressed to win a popularity contest among her co-workers. And, *I,* after all that disgrace, didn't even get invited to the wedding!

The bottom line is not to take yourself or life too seriously. Roll with the punches even if you crack a couple of ribs. When you laugh at yourself, others will laugh with you rather than talk about you viciously behind your back. Whether you're a Southerner, Northerner, Westerner, or European, people have a tendency to snip and gossip. Quickly defuse it by turning it into a joke.

As a young sportswriter, I was among the first women sports reporters in the nation. There were still many barriers to break through and much acceptance to be gained from the male athletes, coaches, and sportswriters. Most locker rooms were still emphatically closed to female reporters. This was fine with me since the only unclothed male I had ever seen was my baby nephew when I changed his diaper. He rewarded my intrusion with a steady stream straight to my face. I always waited very ladylike in my skirt and heels in the weight rooms for the players to come to me.

One night I was on deadline and frantic not to miss a star player I needed to quote in my story. Goaded on by the television guys (they're always the troublemakers), I insisted on going into the visiting Chicago Cubs locker room. Evidently, I was the first woman to make such a request, so much discussion went on while I waited. Finally, a Cubs official appeared at the door and waved me in. I blanched. With head down, I timidly shuffled in, thinking only, "If my daddy could only see me in this *den* of iniquity, he'd kill me."

When I got back to the newspaper, I explained to my crusty sports editor the heroic lengths to which I had gone to secure the interview. He grinned and took a long draw on a cigarette.

"So, you finally went into the locker room, huh?" He started to laugh while my cheeks started to burn. "Well, how was it?"

I shrugged. "It was interesting."

"Really?"

"Yeah, I'll never forget the night I saw my first *bare* Cub," I replied.

Southern women know that successful survival in life calls for a woman to be a chameleon and adapt as necessary. A proper Southern lady would never have entered that locker room. So, a spunky Southern career professional went in her place. Then the proper Southern lady returned to find the situation quite amusing and gained a marvelous story to tell over the years. Even detractors who decried such an act as immoral, unconscionable, and downright insufferable found it rather amusing. Humor is a great equalizer because it makes humble mincemeat out of the most superior and heroes of the meekest while those in between bond by sharing a good laugh.

Share your mishaps with others and put a humorous rather than a grim spin on them. Southerners are great storytellers, so we are occasionally guilty of embellishing a story to make it funnier, but we believe that a hearty laugh justifies the means. We love to entertain and delight those around us.

In dark, depressing times, cheer yourself up by watching a funny movie or reading a humorous book. Tell yourself a funny story that takes you back to a situation or time full of fun and happiness. Call an old friend and laugh over old times. Those terrific "remember when" stories can change a glum mood into a good mood quicker than a banana can turn brown.

In the South, humor is the most sustaining element of our lives and, quite frankly, it is what allows the women of our culture to be steel magnolias. Humor allows us to keep our sanity so that we can deal calmly with the real traumas of life.

By the way, have you heard the joke about why Southern women never participate in group sex?

Because afterwards, there would be too many thank-you notes to write.

CHAPTER TEN

THE TRADITION OF HONORING HOME AND HEARTH

A FEW DAYS BEFORE Christmas one year, an acquaintance approached me in the gym as I was working out.

"Are you, as they say here in the South, *ready* for Christmas?" asked the transplanted Californian with a teasing grin.

I stopped my workout and paused to reflect on what he had said. "Are you ready for Christmas?" is a standard Southern greeting during the holiday season. I, myself, use it dozens of times between Thanksgiving and December 25th. It was obvious that he found great amusement in those words.

"Are you saying that only Southerners use that greeting?" I asked curiously.

"I had *never* heard that expression until I moved to the South," he replied, shaking his head in wonderment.

"That's interesting," I said thoughtfully. "I guess we say that because the holidays are such a big deal for us and we put such effort into decorating, gift buying, baking, parties, and all that."

"That's right," he agreed. "Christmas is a BIG deal in the South. You guys spend six months preparing for it and the other six months recovering from it."

Through the eyes of an outsider, I saw what I had previously taken for granted—holidays are of great importance in the South. *All* holidays. While Christmas is our crowning glory, we are dutiful to celebrations and decorations of big and lesser holidays from Thanksgiving to Memorial Day. Holidays, in short, are a critical part of our steadfast commitment to family, home, and tradition.

Today's Southern woman successfully combines a career with homemaking responsibilities. We nest very well and take extraordinary pride in our homes. For instance, you will never hear a Southern woman proudly proclaim, "I can't even boil water!" Why, such a comment would relegate her to the "undesirables" list by her discriminating, judgmental, and nonforgiving peers!

In the South, family is cherished and honored. Although we love our jobs and are successful at them, our homes and families are more important. We have not chosen to participate in the career world by sacrificing our home lives. And though it can be exhausting, we have not given up on that old-fashioned notion that we can, indeed, have it all. However, we never forget that salaries can be replaced but people, especially family, are irreplaceable.

My friend Bridget works harder at being a good homemaker than anyone I have ever seen. Her home and family are the most cherished parts of her life. Every night, a home-cooked dinner—made completely from scratch—welcomes her husband and children. Despite her hectic daily schedule, she never rearranges her priorities. Her strong focus leads her children to tell everyone about their "supermom."

"You have to work at it," she says with strong conviction. "My husband and my family have to know that they come first in my life. Regardless of how tired I might be, I give them my full attention every evening. It's rarely ever easy, but it's always worthwhile."

This does not mean that we take our careers less seriously than other women. We just take family and home more seriously than most. Happily, we have discovered that we *can* balance home with career, for the best of all worlds. Probably, more than anything else, this attitude separates us from most other women. We are furiously attached to our homes and devoted to creating a loving ambiance of warmth and coziness.

Our peers judge us by our culinary skills, particularly baking and especially biscuit making. You're considered to be a Class A biscuit maker if you can "make your biscuits out by hand" rather than rolling the batter and cutting the biscuits out with a cookie cutter or glass. This is one technique I worked hard to learn from my mother because a biscuit that is pinched off from the dough is a fluffier, lighter biscuit. The more the dough is worked, the tougher the biscuit becomes. Of all the things she has taught me, this is the skill of which I am most proud.

It is important to take time to learn the things that your mother and grandmother know. It is a time-tested secret of the South that we pay homage to tradition and give it eternal life by passing it down through generations. If your mother makes the best lasagna, don't just get the recipe—have her teach you exactly how to make it. My mother always says, "Oh, I don't follow the recipe. I put a pinch of this and a handful of that in." If your mother dies with a special skill or knowledge that you did not learn, that skill dies with her and stops with her generation.

In the South, we don't let that happen.

In Mississippi, there is a story that has circulated since the Civil War of a woman who saved her beloved plantation through the ingenious use of Southern hospitality. She threw open the doors of her home and invited the enemy to a dinner party. While those on neighboring plantations scurried about furiously digging holes in which to bury the family silver and valuables, she ordered that her tables be laid with the finest silver and china and that what little food remained should be gathered for the best feast possible.

Incredulously, her daughters questioned their mother's sanity. But she smiled sweetly and said, "When the Union soldiers arrive on this plantation, they will receive the kindness of our Southern hospitality."

For days, the soldiers had been approaching her home in a steady march, confiscating—or rather downright stealing—possessions of any worth from each home they encountered. Finally the soldiers arrived and when the lady of manor opened the door, she smiled graciously and welcomed the enemy soldiers into her home saying, "Please come in. We've been waiting for you. Please make yourself at home while we prepare a homemade meal for you. I'm certain it's been quite a while since you had a nice home-cooked meal."

The soldiers were obviously taken aback by her graciousness but impressed, nonetheless, by her cool, hospitable demeanor. They ate to their hearts' content and then declined her offer for beds, choosing instead to camp on the veranda. The next morning after breakfast the company's captain thanked her for her hospitality and the troops departed, leaving behind all the silver and china. At the other plantations, they had dug up the earth to uncover treasures, but this time, although the valuables lay in plain view, the soldiers did not take anything.

A short time later, the woman answered a knock at the door to discover a young, sheepish-looking Union soldier. In his hands, he held a couple of pieces of her silver that she had not realized were missing.

"Won't you come in?" she asked with a smile.

"No, ma'am. My captain sent me back to bring you these. He said there is no way that we could take anything from a hospitable lady like you."

Southern women cherish their homes and will do anything to preserve and protect their beloved hearths, even if it means cunningly wooing the enemy. We call it "killing them with kindness and homemade cobbler." The citizens of Savannah, Georgia, made history when they used their hospitality to deter General Sherman from burning that beautiful city on his fiery march through the state. Having heard what had happened to Atlanta, Savannah officials met Sherman on the road before he got to the town, welcomed him graciously, and gifted him with the city. And, thus, their hospitality spared the historic beauty of Georgia's first city.

Throughout the South, our homes are filled with warmth and attention to detail. The desire to have perfectly detailed homes is so great that one magazine, *Southern Living,* has developed an entire cottage industry by supplying the latest trends in decorating, gardening, and cooking exclusively to Southern subscribers. To many, it is the Southern homemakers' bible.

In short, we are serious about our homes and we are dedicated to carrying on the tradition of Southern hospitality. No one ever enters my mother's home without being offered food and drink, or rather *partaking* of food and drink. She will not hush until the guests have at least enjoyed coffee and a piece of homemade cake. They have no choice because my mother does not run a home of democracy, she runs one that is presided over by a grandmotherly dictator.

When the visit ends, she, like many other Southern women, will round up things for the guests to take home—a jar of homemade jam, a mess of green beans (a mess, in the unlikely event you *don't know,* is a Southern term for "enough for one meal"), or fresh, garden-grown tomatoes. My mother does not do well taking "no" for an answer. When I visit her, a typical conversation will go something like this:

"I cooked your favorite—fried green tomatoes. Do you want to eat some?" she'll ask.

"No, thank you. I'd love to, but I'm on a diet."

"Well, you have to eat something, and fried green tomatoes won't hurt you. They have lots of vitamins and other things you need to stay alive." This is her favorite argument.

"I really appreciate it, but I'll pass this time. Thank you."

This goes back and forth for several minutes until she eventually appears with a plate of fried green tomatoes, shoves the plate in front of me, and says firmly, "Here. You eat these. Your stomach is going to grow together if you don't start eating something." Then, she launches into an endless story of a woman she knew once who died from her insides growing together because she didn't eat. I guess that woman didn't have a mother who knew how to fry green tomatoes. Or maybe *she* had a mother who understood the meaning of "no, thank you."

The center of activity in the Southern home is the kitchen where the family congregates and visitors, more often than not, enter through the kitchen door. Southern families spend so much time in the kitchen that it has become popular for new homes to have kitchens that are completely opened to the family room so that constant conversation can flow easily between the two rooms.

From these kitchens the tantalizing smells of home-cooked meals flow from the stoves, not microwaves. Sundays are an occasion for huge family affairs where dinner (in the South, lunch is called dinner; dinner is called supper) consists of fried chicken, banana pudding, and homemade biscuits. And, usually, preachers are brought home to bless the food and eat a chicken leg.

Southern ministers are required to possess a love for fried chicken. You cannot preach the gospel to a Southern congregation if you are a vegetarian. It is not allowed. Until recent years, it was agreed among congregations that part of the pastor's salary was Sunday dinner with one of the church families. Each member family took a turn hosting the preacher and his family. I heard a minister in Nashville commiserate once during a sermon about all the fried chicken he had eaten at Sunday dinners by relating a story he had heard from a fellow pastor.

"I thought you could always count on having fried chicken for dinner, until I heard of a pastor's visit to one home. He said to the youngest child, 'I bet I know what we're having for dinner.' The little boy flashed a snaggle-tooth smile slyly as if he knew a secret the minister did not. He said, 'Betcha can't!'

"The preacher said confidently, 'Fried chicken.' The child shook his head firmly. 'Nope.'

"The pastor ventured uncertainly, 'Roast beef.' The little boy laughed delightedly. 'You can't guess, so I'll tell ya. We're having buzzard!'

"The preacher was stumped and said, 'Buzzard! Surely, son, you have misunderstood.'

"The little boy shook his head furiously. 'No, sir, I didn't. I heard Mama tell Daddy on the way to church this morning, 'Well, we gotta have that old buzzard for dinner today. We might as well have him this Sunday as next!' "

We highly prize a beautifully decorated, comfortable home with fresh flowers, candles, and an inviting fire. Our homes smell wonderful, creating the difference between a good and great environment. Magnolias, jasmine, and honeysuckle vines grace our yards while fresh flowers and simmering pots of potpourri scent our homes. Southern women smell delicious and so do our homes.

Judy's husband, Donald, gave new meaning to bringing flowers to his wife a couple of years ago. She had mentioned in passing that she would love to have some brightly colored azaleas. A few days later, she came home to find a yard planted full of azalea plants, a gift from her doting husband. Judy is one of those perfect Southern women who hand-makes sugary orchids to top homemade wedding cakes and would never dream of using a store-bought pie shell. She is just a little *too* perfect, if you ask me, but I hang around with her anyway because I have some kind of strange fascination with viewing perfection in the flesh.

There are those who say that you can't go home again. Even one prominent Southern writer claimed such, but he was a man and I suspect that Southern men do not attach the same sentiment to home that Southern women do. For that reason and from my own experience, I must disagree. You can always go home again. Of course, things change, but the essence of what home means remains constant.

In the South, our love for the soil, where our hearts are firmly planted, is legendary. Almost unexplainable. My great-grandfather, who owned hundreds, probably thousands, of acres of land, died long before my birth. Yet, when my feet touch the soil upon which once trod the feet of a man I never knew but whose blood courses through my veins, my heart is filled with a resurgence of spirit that is exhilarating and uplifting. As I view the majestic beauty of hardwood trees and sparkling streams from a mountaintop of his once proud domain, I feel I have come home.

As surely as the sparkling water that winds seductively through those gorgeous mountains, my blood pulses in that red Georgia clay. Southern women are deeply wedded to the traditions and generations that have gone before them. The word *home* is never taken lightly but, rather, it is taken to heart.

By the same token, home is where I escape to when life becomes too difficult and too hard to understand. I am always resuscitated by a visit to a grass-bare spot under a maple tree that angles crookedly over the rippling creek behind the home where I grew up. It was under this tree that I spent many hours. It was where I wrote my first words, dreamed my first big dreams, read Nancy Drew mysteries, and later cried the first tears of a brokenhearted teenager after my boyfriend dumped me. I had repeatedly "conducted myself like a lady" as my mother had often instructed and after that heartbreak, I wasn't sure that my mother really did know best, after all. That maple tree, so beautiful in the fall with its dripping red leaves, knows my tears, dreams, and prayers as well as I do.

When I am brutalized by life's arrows, I grab my down-filled bed pillow and head for Mama's house where I welcome the smell of turnip greens cooking on the stove (a somewhat foul smell usually detested by me) just as I am welcomed. After a visit to the creek and my maple tree followed by a good night's sleep in my own bed, I am ready, once again, to tackle a sometimes uncertain life.

We Southern women know that the homes of our yesterdays are the backbone of our todays and the special memories for our tomorrows. With that in mind, we cling feverishly and respectfully to the past. It is the sacred homage for tradition that deeply roots our commitment to hospitality and warmth.

Warm homes and beautiful memories are created when you:

Get to the heart of the matter. Make family your heart and cherish them—even the errant, thoughtless ones!

Keep your priorities straight. Make people, rather than possessions, your top priority because life, once it is gone, cannot be revived.

Treasure your hearth. Plant flowers, either in your yard or in pots for your balcony. Warm a room with a fire, soft lighting, and tantalizing smells that drift from the kitchen, even if it only means brewing hazelnut-flavored coffee.

Make your home smell wonderful. Place fragrant plants in your yard and fresh flowers in your home. Use simmering pots of potpourri.

Find extra time to devote to special things. Home-cook meals, using a stove, not a microwave. Learn to bake and do it with love.

Decorate with love and attention. Coordinate the furnishings of your home as carefully as you do your clothes.

Learn to sew. If nothing else, master the ability to sew on buttons and hem skirts. These are very important skills for a good nester. Georgia-born Joanne Woodward is the quintessential Southern woman. On the evening that Hollywood presented her with the Best Actress Oscar® for *The Three Faces of Eve,* she was wearing a strapless satin gown that she had sewn herself. She has also succeeded in staying married for over forty years to Paul Newman, one of the most desired men in the world. Ms. Woodward is a terrific example of a Southern woman who believes it is possible to have it all—a lasting marriage, a closely knit family, and an award-winning career. She has proven that you do not have to sacrifice one of these for any of the others.

Learn handicrafts such as needlepoint. In the South, knitting, crocheting, and quilting are considered forms of art.

Collect family heirlooms. They keep you close to your important past.

Record your family history. It only takes three generations to lose track of the people and events that have gone before you.

Take special time to learn the things your mother knows. If your mother dies with a special skill or knowledge that you did not learn, that skill dies with her and stops with her generation.

Be respectful of others and traditions. In most places throughout the South, a funeral procession is treated with tremendous respect. Drivers pull their cars over to the side of the road and come to a complete stop. Traffic doesn't move until the procession passes. Pedestrians stop and bow their heads in reverence until the hearse and its parade of cars passes. Newcomers to the South are driven crazy by this tradition, but it is our way of honoring the life of a fellow Southerner. Even if we never knew him or her.

The Southern lifestyle is an incredible blend of progress, history, and tradition. While Southerners are proud of the corporate skyscrapers that dot the metro landscape from Charlotte to Atlanta to Dallas, we treasure the antebellum mansions and homesteads of our past and those historic moments that remind us that important lessons in life are not always easily or quickly learned. Because of the sweat, toil, and spilled blood of our ancestors, we know that home and family should always be the epicenter of our lives. It is what we have believed for two centuries. It is what we continue to practice—old-fashioned traditions in a modern, fast-paced world.

CHAPTER ELEVEN

Life's a Peach

SOUTHERN WOMEN are not perfect. No, seriously, we're not. But we are perfectly comfortable with making mistakes and learning from them. It doesn't daunt us at all or play havoc with our self-esteem. We accept errors, often laugh at them, and basically just attack life with optimism and unswerving determination.

Of course, life isn't peachy. It is marred by mistakes, but making mistakes is part of our most valuable education in life. They are the vines from which grow our grapes of wisdom. They provide the story line for all those great parables and proverbs, which is one reason that Southerners deal so well with mistakes. We love to have a great story to tell.

My dear friend Debbie is a terrific example of a Southern woman who turned an overripe peach into a peach of a situation and, in the bargain, produced a wonderful story for us to tell.

Debbie had both the good fortune *and* the misfortune to be born into a great motor-sports family. It was good because the family's racing ventures produced a successful business and a comfortable lifestyle for them. It was not so good because as the only progeny of such high-powered, successful parents, she was expected to work in the family business.

Few women have ever been born smarter or possessed of a keener marketing savvy than Miss Academia, star of her high-school and college classes. Since the family owned one of the nation's most respected race car tracks, after she earned a degree in business, she dutifully reported to the family track for work as its marketing director.

I found myself in constant awe of the knack that she possessed for marketing and promotion. With Debbie in the position, the track gained greater renown, won awards, and grew even more successful. Yet, she was not happy. Responsible and devoted as a daughter, yes. Happy as a person, no.

Did I mention that Debbie, despite being only five feet four, had attended college on a basketball scholarship? She's quite a scrapper. In many ways. From her father, she had inherited a shrewd business acumen *and* an athletic agility. Her dad, a Southern stock car racing legend, had won over 1,200 races in his career before becoming a track owner.

So, Debbie began to develop a plan. She knew she was responsible for her own happiness and while there were some things she couldn't control, there were others that she could. If working in racing was what she must do, then she, by golly, would have fun.

Debbie became a race car driver. One of the best.

I was there the night that my dear, sweet friend won her first race. I clapped until my hands hurt and cheered until my voice grew hoarse. She took her victory lap, then pulled up for the winner's circle presentation. Debbie climbed out of the car, removed her helmet, and shook her head to release the cascade of bright blond hair that fell inches past her shoulders. That was just the first of many wins for her en route to capturing a couple of driving championships.

That night, when Debbie triumphed over more than twenty-five or thirty male drivers, she won a major victory in life, too. She discovered that the secret to enjoying life is to blend the good with the bad. The parable? Great triumphs are often ignited from the smoking embers of a blazing defeat. The key is to fan the flames.

Southern women treat life like a basket of peaches that has overripened and started to develop unsavory bruises. We appreciatively pick out the good peaches and then deal with the rotting fruit. Then, we tackle each peach on a peach-by-peach basis. We carve out the rotten spots, dispose of the pits, salvage the good pieces, then drag out cartons of thick, rich cream and make homemade ice cream (have you noticed how much we like to eat in the South? It is, in short, our salvation). Waste not, want not, Mother always chirps. With that kind of mentality, we refuse to throw away pieces of our lives that were riddled with mistakes. Just as with peaches, we salvage the good, learn from the bad.

A few years ago while on a business trip to North Carolina, I stumbled across a newspaper classified ad that clearly illustrated one Southern woman's resiliency. The ad read:

For Sale: Satin Wedding Dress Covered in Lace. Size 8. Worn Once. By Mistake.

Humor, as I have explained, is very important for survival in the South. Levity renews our strength. But it is not as important as our dedication to learning from the hard times and the evil people we encounter in our lives. Okay, so I've already said that, but it is such a vital part of the creed by which we live that redundancy is necessary to underscore our dedication to that belief.

I am as grateful for the torturous Satans who have darkened my path as I am for the saints who have lighted the way. I have learned as much—sometimes more—from my enemies as I have from the mentors who lovingly taught and educated me. Our detractors are particularly adept at illuminating our faults and flaws. In fact, they just outright point them out to us and sometimes offer to draw a map so that we'll be certain to understand just how imperfect we are. Our enemies teach us survival skills and help us to see how strong and resilient we really are. In short, we learn a lot from them. So, see, everyone has a purpose in life. Even mean people.

Southerners do not run from trouble. We stay and fight. In fact, we're legendary for it. Strong numbers of Southerners have enthusiastically participated in every war fought on American or foreign soil, beginning with the American Revolutionary War. In fact, Tennessee is called the Volunteer State because of the vast numbers of volunteers sent by that state to the Revolutionary War, War of 1812, Mexican War, and the Civil War. Obviously, if there's a good fight going on, a Southern man hates to miss it.

It is this kind of feisty spirit that anchors the South and its people. Especially the women. But remember: the greatest battle you will wage in life is against that of cynicism. That horrible little voice that whispers, "Life stinks" and "People are out for their own good. Trust no one." Cynicism takes more away from our lives than it ever gives. Southern women fight a constant battle against it, but we refuse to allow an abundance of cynicism to cloud the optimistic existence that we love.

Optimism encourages the creation of dreams and fuels our desire to follow those dreams. In the South, we are great dreamers. We are also great doers. The combination of dreaming and doing lies at the center of our success, while plucky tenacity feeds our never-say-die attitude.

Are there dreams that lie stifled within your heart? Dreams that you hold dear but have found neither the time nor inclination to make come true? Sometimes you can be so busy making a living that you forget to make the life you really want for yourself. And when that happens, you have let yourself down.

Begin today to follow your dream because the day that your dreams come true will be the greatest day of your life—the day that makes all the other days of upsets, disappointments, frustrations, and heartbreaks worth all the agony. For it is that day—the day on which your dream comes true—that adds the greatest glimmer and sparkle to your life.

Mistakes and the lessons learned from them prepare you to chase your dreams. The bigger the dreams, the more preparation it takes. Southern women gracefully accept mistakes and put diligent effort into learning from them. I've made many mistakes, and most of them taught me a great deal.

I made a mistake once when, as a sportswriter, I wrote a newspaper column about the new football coach at a top university. I was certain it would win an award. In the column, I likened the new coach, who faced disgruntled athletes and fans, to David in the lions' den. I congratulated myself on a brilliant analogy. I was still feeling pretty cocky the next day when the paper's general editor stuck his head in the door of my office.

"Good column," he said, giving me a thumbs-up.

I smiled smugly. "Thanks."

He started to walk off, but stopped. He turned back to face me with a puzzled, pensive look. "You know, I don't know a lot about the Bible," he started slowly, which was an understatement since he was an agnostic. "But I *think* it was *Daniel* in the lions' den, not David."

Suffice it to say, I did not win an award. Wasn't even nominated.

However, as with peaches, Southern women do not accept any situation as being a total loss. We make jam and jelly out of fruit that others would throw away. We staunchly believe in making the best out of bad situations.

My mother is tremendously resourceful, stubbornly persistent, and will never give up as long as there is a roll of masking tape to be found. When she runs out of clear tape, she wraps presents with that ugly beige masking tape. She believes that it can fix many problems in life. And, to put it mildly, she was in absolute heaven when that sturdy, metal-colored tape, called duct tape, was invented because she had yet another way to mend the boo-boos of life. We tease her outrageously about this tape passion of hers, but to be quite honest, I can recall vividly two occasions when she used masking tape to repair what the medical profession proclaimed unfixable.

Once a severely crippled calf was born in my dad's herd of cattle. The poor creature's front legs were bent back against its stomach and, to complicate matters, the bottoms of its front hooves had not developed pads. Without those pads, the hooves were too tender to support any weight. So, if the calf could have straightened its legs to stand, its hooves could not have taken the pressure.

The veterinarian had struggled to deliver the calf and save its mother. But when he saw the deformed baby, he shook his head.

"We need to go ahead and put this calf to sleep. There's no way that those legs will ever straighten out or that she can survive. No way."

Daddy agreed, but for some reason added, "Let's wait until tomorrow when you come back to check on the mama."

As soon as the two men left, my mother scurried out to the barn carrying her beloved masking tape, two twelve-inch wooden rulers, bandages, and a pair of tiny socks. She tenderly straightened the calf's legs, swaddled the hooves and legs in white bandages, and taped them tightly. Then, she broke the rulers into halves and used them as splints, which she wrapped tightly with tape and more bandaging and then more tape. She completed the ensemble with the socks. Then, with the help of my brother, she carried the ailing animal over to its mother and held it so that it could suckle its nourishment. Cautiously, the calf tried its first steps and, lo and behold, it walked.

The next day, the vet returned and was both amused and surprised at mother's doctoring attempts. Gently, he tried to reason with one of the most unreasonable women in the world.

"You've done a very good job, but I am afraid that you're wasting your time. There is no way that calf can live. You need to allow me to put her down. It's for the best," he implored.

My mother stood firmly and obstinately. "No. I will try everything I can. My efforts may not be successful, but *I will not give up.*" Spoken like a true Southern woman who refuses to accept defeat easily. Sometimes defeat is inevitable, but it is never accepted with good humor or graciousness by otherwise gracious women. Defeat is fought every step of the way. Southerners have a particular aversion to defeat. We don't much cotton to it, which explains why some folks are still mad about that surrender in 1865.

Oh, about the calf. Thanks to my stubborn mother and her roll of masking tape, the calf grew up to have straight legs, padded hooves, and to be one of the strongest in the herd. My mother defied conventional medical wisdom and turned what looked like a mistake into a celebration of life. Her efforts serve as a reminder to me as to why I should never give up, even when it looks as though there is no other choice. Always hold out with a little hope, faith, and perseverance.

A couple of decades later, Mom's masking tape defied medical science again. She was stricken with Bell's palsy, a temporary facial paralysis that can and normally does cause permanent drooping of the affected area. The doctor assured her that the paralysis would disappear, but he cautioned there was a 90 percent chance that her mouth would be pulled permanently to one side. Again, that stubborn woman refused to listen. She went right home, got out her masking tape, and used it to pull her face back to its proper position. For two weeks she walked around looking like the victim of a face-lift gone terribly wrong. She even wore the tape to church, to the amusement of the rest of congregation. But it worked. When the removed the tape, her mouth was centered, straight, and, to Daddy's disappointment, worked as rapidly as it always had.

It is successes like these that make Southern women believe in their own power and ability to overcome odds and to make dreams come true. Every time you encounter adversity and conquer it, you gain more confidence in your ability to overcome tribulations and to make dreams come true.

There isn't a woman alive who hasn't chosen to be in a relationship with what turns out to be the wrong man and then later expressed remorse over that mistake. I wish I had only made that kind of mistake once! However, I never consider it a mistake but an important lesson.

I once briefly regretted that a relationship had not ended twelve months before it did. I rationalized that it would have saved both of us, particularly me, a great deal of disappointment and hurt. Then, when I got into the proper Southern-woman train of thought, I realized that the last twelve months of the relationship were the most important, although they had been the unhappiest. I enjoyed the first years of the relationship, but I *learned* from the last year. Those final twelve months made me a stronger, wiser person with greater depth and understanding. Had I walked away earlier, I would have left a great deal of knowledge behind. In life, there are really no mistakes, just important opportunities for learning.

Southern women make a conscious effort to believe the best. But when we can no longer believe in someone's innate goodness, we just get even. Now, let me stress that it takes a whole lot to get us to the point of seeking revenge, but when that time comes, just stand back. It is not a pretty sight. It means that our patience—which is often and appropriately compared to that of a saint—has run out.

Mostly, we realize that life requires a lot of patience if you are to get what you really want. Southern women are very patient. We wait years to get the man we want and years to dump him if that becomes necessary. We are very patient about revenge or giving someone her comeuppance. Positioning, we realize, is most important. Our benevolence disappears, we look out only for Number One, and start carving out those rotten spots on the peaches.

Southern women are smart enough to be frightened of other Southern women when that carving time comes. In fact, an infuriated Southern woman makes Genghis Khan look like an angel. Her revenge is insidious, painstakingly strategic, and deceptively hidden beneath charm and manners. I assure you that if a Southern woman ever decides to drive a stake through your heart, you will not see it coming and then, chances are, her name will never appear on your list of suspects. Her charm will make it impossible to finger her as the vindictive vigilante. Plus, her patience will put a lot of time between your repeated offenses and her singularly spectacular act of revenge. More than likely, you will long have forgotten all the injustices you did to her. You will believe she has forgiven and completely forgotten.

And that, my friend, will be the biggest mistake you ever make.

Here is a tale of very small vengeance but, nonetheless, a good example. I once got a very bad haircut from an extremely rude hairdresser. Not only was it disgracefully bad; it was expensive. Plus, since my schedule is always overbooked, I was sickened at my loss of time as well as the money. I was angry that I would have to go back for a second appointment for him to administer first aid to a disaster. I arrived exactly on time and went back to his cubicle. He looked up from the unsuspecting client on whom he was either wreaking havoc or weaving magic to snarl hatefully at me.

"It's going to be an hour before I get to you."

I was genuinely puzzled. "I'm sorry, did I write down the appointment wrong? I thought it was for two-thirty."

"No," he snapped. "You got the time right, but I'm running behind."

Furious but without a word, I wheeled around and left. I never went back, but two years later, I called the salon and using another name, booked a two-hour appointment for a cut, color, manicure, and pedicure for the Saturday before Mother's Day, the busiest day of the year. Since I did not show up, the hairdresser and his salon lost a lot of income. Financially, I didn't get my money back, but emotionally, I hit pay dirt with that piece of revenge.

Oh, and by the way. The name and phone number I used to book the appointment? It was that of the treacherous female who stole my boyfriend away when I was in the eleventh grade. Awww, it's so sweet when you can avenge two wrongs in one shot!

Life isn't always a peach, but you can make a great ambrosia from it. Remember these tips:

- Hard times enable us to grow. So, embrace them, welcome then, and recognize their value.
- Our greatest lessons come from our enemies. Learn from them and then, if necessary, get even.
- Patience is patently necessary in life for enjoyment, fulfillment, and revenge.

- Southern women sometimes play dumb. We may know our man is cheating or lying, but we wait until we have a file full of information before *he* knows that we know. Then, it's all over but the shouting.
- Scorned Southern women rarely require the services of a private detective. We are quite ingenious and capable of doing the work ourselves. We check the redial on the phone, the daily mileage on his car, the phone numbers in his pager. We believe in knowing exactly what is going on before we make decisions that dramatically impact our lives.
- Mistakes and the lessons they teach are the stepping-stones to dreams that come true. Every heartbreak or mishap will give birth to a wonderful blessing.
- Use resourcefulness and ingenuity to make the best of a bad situation.
- Always settle the score. Those who betray us in life never rest completely easy again. It may be years down the road, but we always right the wrong that's been done—and always in a ladylike manner.

The bottom line is that life is what you make of it. In the South, the code of honor requires thoughtfulness and kindness. It also demands that you do unto others as has been done unto you. Good or bad. When someone takes advantage and steps over the line, we send him or her hurtling back over the line. Territorial protection is crucial to survival, and we Southerners know how to survive at all cost. Proper Southern women never strike the first blow, but we *usually* strike the last one.

Southern women simply deal with life. We fight through

the difficult times, adore the happy times, and refuse to taint the good times with memories of the bad times and bad people.

And, it doesn't hurt if you have a roll or two of masking tape on hand.

CHAPTER TWELVE

Better Buy a Roll of Tums: Someone Wicked This Way Comes

All women are naturally intuitive. We see, sense, and know things that never occur to men. While all women are blessed with this gift, Southern women are almost witchlike in their use of this sacred subliminal knowledge. Since we are crafty enough to realize its extraordinary benefits, we consciously fine-tune it to sheer perfection.

My mother, a perfect example of a Southern sorceress, is so uncannily accurate that there are times I could swear that she has a crystal ball she consults. From her, as well as through many missteps in my own judgment, I learned to fine-tune my intuition almost to her scarylike proportions. Without question, any woman can cleverly enhance this natural gift with just a little attention to detail. Although it is helpful in all situations, it is particularly useful in spotting troublemakers and manipulative people—the very ones who wreak havoc in otherwise serene lives and introduce you to a troublesome malady known as ulcers.

Every woman, at one time or another, has shuddered and remarked, "He gives me the creeps. I have a very bad feeling about him"—and with that insight, turned and retreated to a far corner away from the villainous character. Other times, we've welcomed these men into our lives with open hearts and open arms, only to learn the bitter truth too late. Or, we trusted a co-worker who turned out to be as venomous and deadly as the asp that Cleopatra clutched to her breast.

Why does intuition work one time and not another? Because we see what we want to see. When we take the time to look deeper, we discover a wealth of information that guides us in making sensible, not senseless, decisions. A woman's intuition never fails her. It does not work, however, when she has switched it off and is oblivious of the signals radiating from her soul. Otherwise, it is a sensitive radar that is right on target every time.

Use your intuition to quickly spot a manipulative person who will try to control your life and destiny while looking out for her own best interests. From a husband who abuses, to a mother who controls, to a scheming co-worker, manipulators can destroy your self-esteem and spoon out torturous punishment. Strong self-esteem, you'll recall, is the key to a successful Southern woman.

One of the greatest stresses faced in the workplace is that of scheming co-workers who delight in keeping their prey thrown off balance. When this type of person undermines your self-confidence, she has attacked your ability to excel and prosper. Don't let it happen. Snatch control of your life away from this kind of person.

Interestingly enough, we Southern women are sometimes accused of being manipulative simply because we employ our charm to change minds or situations. Actually, we use all our skills to manage a situation to achieve a more desirable outcome, but we are never completely self-centered in our mission. We prefer everything to work out to everyone's benefit. Manipulative people, however, are wicked instigators who are interested in only winning for themselves—at any and all costs to others. They are dangerous because they work without the guidance of a moral or ethical conscience. They are particularly deadly when they are convinced of their own self-righteousness—which is most of the time.

The majority of Southern women are supremely self-confident. One reason is that we have learned to use our womanly intuition to ward off manipulators who threaten our happiness as well as our physical and emotional well-being. This extraordinary gift wasn't just dumped in our laps. It takes much effort and many years to develop this intuition to state-of-the-art perfection. As a woman, you are born with basic instinct; now here's how to enhance it.

Intuition is enhanced by experience. We Southern women learn from the trials and tribulations in our lives and the mistakes we make—particularly the people we wrongly trust. That's why we are usually in our late twenties or so before we fully hit our intuitive stride. You have to live life to learn it and consciously absorb the experiences to benefit from the knowledge. As you approach middle age, you will realize that much of your intuition is based on experience and lessons you have learned. It is crucial to weave those lessons into your intuitive subconscious because those experiences then act as a database that programs your reactions, judgments, and choices.

I got caught napping once with my intuition completely turned off. It was a valuable lesson, although it served up a tremendous amount of hurt and disillusionment. I would give up my Coca-Cola stock before I would give up what I learned from that situation (by the way, that's saying a lot since Georgians are notorious for hoarding and rarely selling the stock of the soft-drink company that made Atlanta famous).

I once worked with a woman generally considered to be a good though somewhat boring employee and dependable despite a strong tendency for procrastination. By all appearances, she was simply one of those faithful employees who showed up for work every day, went into her office quietly, and plugged away at her work until it was time to go home.

There were no visible indications that she was a troublemaker. Since political battles were always raging in the company, I tried to determine who was friend or foe. I decided that she was neither—not to be counted on as an ally, but never cunning enough to be an enemy. Basically, I just considered her too lazy to go to the trouble.

WRONG.

I should have recalled my grandmother's warning that "still waters run deep." She said always to beware of the quiet ones because they're the ones whose minds are constantly working since they're not using them to run their mouths. My colleague's treachery caught me so completely off guard that for once in my life, I was absolutely speechless when her pernicious behavior was exposed. That should tell you how unexpected it was.

When the truth was revealed to me, it was quite a sobering moment. I had considered the woman to be innocuous and nonthreatening. While I had kept my eyes fixed on the openly dangerous, bloodthirsty wolves, I was blind to the insidious mouse who scampered around surreptitiously. Yet, she had been the root of many problems and conflicts that plagued and baffled me. I could not figure out where all the trouble was starting. When I located the source, I was stunned.

It's true—we are sometimes our own worst enemy. I certainly was in that case because I turned my back and turned off my intuition. I was so intent on keeping an eye on the big, vicious animals that I completely ignored the hungry little mouse who was desperate for a piece of the cheese. Turn on your intuition and tune in to everyone, particularly the most seemingly innocent ones.

It is cynical to say "never trust anyone," but it is realistic to say "rarely trust *completely*." Hold back some trust in order to protect yourself. When you trust completely, your intuition goes to sleep and you're left on the battlefield without a weapon.

Teach yourself to quickly spot the characteristics of a manipulator. The first rule is that most manipulators are women. It takes a lot of skill and cunning to selfishly maneuver things, so I guess men just aren't interested in the time and effort required. However, if you ever meet a manipulative man, run hard and fast, because he can and will be meaner and more evil than a manipulative female. I have only met two manipulative men in my life, but it was like dancing with the devil while the fires of hell licked at my backside.

Manipulative people have a pattern of behavior that makes them easy to spot when you turn on your intuition. Initially, they seek to get their way through charm, flattery, and even gifts. They are unflinchingly persistent and cleverly enticing. They have to work hard at it, unlike Southern women who effortlessly charm and entice. The major difference between Southern women and ruthless manipulators when it comes to charm and flattery is that Southern women use charm and flattery on *everyone.* A manipulator employs these wiles relentlessly on one or two special targets (those who can help her), yet with everyone else she is either casually friendly or coolly aloof.

If the effort of charm is completely exhausted to no avail, they move on to arguing, crying, pouting, or sulking. When that doesn't work, they then try to manipulate you by using a third person such a boss, child, or friend. How many times have you seen a woman manipulatively use a child during a divorce? A manipulator will use every channel of influence and person of power he or she can find.

If you still resist, they move into the more dangerous level. This is the stage of screaming, insults, threats, and slight violence such as throwing things or slapping. Most people, particularly tortured spouses, capitulate and again the manipulator wins. If there is no capitulation at this point, one of two things will happen. Either the manipulator will give up and slink away, or the situation will escalate to the very advanced stage of evil, violence, and destruction.

When you learn to recognize the pattern of a manipulator, your intuition will spring into action and loudly sound the alarm at the first sniff of smoke. Following your intuition can prevent much heartbreak and aggravation.

Be alert to everything around you. It is important always to know what is lurking in the shadows. Heighten your senses to detect all the sounds, smells, and sights around you. Once you develop this knack, you'll be surprised at how often you hear something that embeds itself in your subconscious but doesn't rise to the surface until your intuition calls for it. A seemingly harmless comment that someone makes in passing and means nothing at the time suddenly becomes the crucial clue to a mystery at a later date. We all know how to turn off someone we don't want to listen to. We just close our minds and think about something else while mumbling, "Hmmmm-huh." Do that in reverse by turning off the thoughts that distract when someone is speaking. In other words, don't become self-absorbed. Listen to what is being said. Watch carefully what is being done. These small clues may be valuable in the future.

Take snapshots with your mind. Everything you see—license plates, phone numbers, etc.—are somewhere on the hard drive of your mind. Close your eyes, relax, and think of nothing else except the phone number you want to remember. Don't think so hard, though, that you drive it away. Just relax and focus. In a very short time, it will float to the front of your mind. The harder you try to remember, the more your mind actually suppresses it because you are thinking of too many other things. When you try to remember someone's name, you'll think, "What is his name? It is a simple name." Then, you'll start running through simple names like Tom, John, Jim. This distracts you from remembering.

Practice good memory. In order to retain something in your memory bank, concentrate on it for ten seconds. After a phone call or other conversation, take a moment to replay it in your mind. You'll be surprised how much you remember. Taking the time to write something down embeds it further in your mind. Even if you lose the note, chances are you'll remember it. Doing two things at one time prohibits good memory. For instance, addressing envelopes during a phone conversation will distract you from remembering much about either activity. There are many who will tell you that a Southern woman never forgets.

Listen quickly but carefully. Don't let someone be on the third sentence of a story while you are still running the first sentence through your mind. Follow each word of each sentence as if you were proofreading a letter. Your mind will absorb those words, and you can later hit the playback button and analyze it more in depth.

Pay attention to all details—no matter how minor. The strongest clues to the largest mysteries lie in the smallest details. One friend discovered her husband had a girlfriend because she was alert, listened quickly but carefully, and paid attention to all details. It was one tiny detail that wretchedly derailed his train. He came home one night chatting with great animation about an old female acquaintance he had seen. She had experienced some recent woes and, stupidly, he thought there was nothing wrong in sharing the story.

The wife, never known for having an ounce of jealousy in her body, listened compassionately to the story. When he finished, she remarked, "That's too bad. I hope that everything will work out for her." Suddenly, it occurred to her that it was unusual that he should have run into this woman by accident since they did not travel in the same circles.

"When was the last time you saw her," she asked out of curiosity.

"I don't know," he shrugged. "Probably six or seven years ago."

"Where did you see her this time?"

"Oh, she's working at the GMC dealership selling trucks."

That tiny detail, which seemed to mean nothing to the husband, meant a great deal to the wife, even a wife renowned for her wholehearted trust.

"The GMC dealership?" she repeated in a puzzled tone. "Hmmm-huh."

"What were you doing at the GMC dealership?"

"I was looking at trucks. I test-drove one."

Now, the cat was completely out of the bag, since the husband was a staunch buyer of Ford vehicles and had never owned a General Motors product in his life. He had often harped on his preference for Ford products and declared that he would never own a GM car or truck. The wife's mind was spinning rapidly. Her intuition based on this one tiny detail told her that something was seriously wrong.

"But you always drive Fords! What in the world possessed you to test-drive a GMC truck?"

"I've changed my mind. This year's models look pretty good. I really like them."

She dropped the conversation, but her mind did not drop the subject. And then, like any dutiful Southern wife, she checked his pager and billfold that night while he was in the shower. She found the phone number for the GMC dealership twice on the pager and the woman's private home phone number scrawled across the back of her business card that was tucked in his billfold. Her intuition was right, and it was the first step in a journey of discoveries that ended in a judge's chambers.

Don't use the "bad memory" excuse to bail out. It's true. Some people have stronger memories than others. But do not accept that you have a weak memory and let it go at that. What memory you have, regardless of how good or bad it is, can be improved by conscious and diligent effort.

Women are blessed with the wonderful natural gift of intuition. Yet, it is given to us in a very embryonic form, far from the powerful epic form it can assume. It takes time, nurturing, attention, and experience for it to develop to the strong, robust stage that makes it a woman's best friend—the kind of friend who never lets you down in a crunch. Southern women know the value of a perfectly tuned intuition and, because of that, we guard it and protect it like the gold in Fort Knox, Kentucky. Probably better.

CHAPTER THIRTEEN

SPIT IN THE DEVIL'S FACE EVEN IF IT ISN'T NICE MANNERS

WHEN THE CHIPS are down and we're backed into a corner, Southern women shed the manners and lace and turn into something akin to runaway chain saws. We fight tooth and acrylic nail for what is ours and what is right. We are not easily defeated or discouraged.

Because adversity shows its ugly face in every facet of every life, there is nothing to do other than rise above and overcome it. Personally, adversity can strengthen and deepen relationships while, professionally, it can be turned into the best promotion-getter in the world. Managers promote employees who deal well with adversity, who solve problems rather than complain about them. Employees who are emotionally tough and determined make life easier for management, so why wouldn't they be promoted quickly to jobs with greater responsibility? When a problem arises, approach your boss with the problem *and* the solution. Ingenuity such as this will take you far in today's business world. Running from adversity will not.

This is the primary reason that Southern women are highly successful career women—the formidable scrappiness that served our ancestors so well in personal fights for survival transferred easily into today's cutthroat corporate environment. The same fortitude that guided my grandmother through the bleak Depression years while she struggled to feed nine children sustains me in a business world riddled with manipulators, liars, and untrustworthy opponents. Inarguably, it takes tremendous strength for a woman to survive, much less prosper, in the corporate world today.

Southern women are not shrinking violets and, contrary to myth, we do not swoon with the vapors when trouble descends. We don't jump into the midst of a fight until we know that it cannot be settled in any other way. But when we must fight, we do. Rare is the Southern woman who does not confront problems head-on when necessary but pretends that if she ignores a problem it will go away. If you encounter a Southern woman like this, know she is a wimp and so is the man to whom she is married—if a man is stupid enough to marry her. A man's man, the kind coveted by lovely Southern belles, is attracted to strong, independent women, not sniffling imitations. And truly invincible Southern women, normally gracious and well mannered, do not hesitate to spit in the devil's face and defy misfortune when it dares to intrude into their lives. It is simply a matter of participating in your destiny rather than being controlled by it.

My friend Jill shared recently the story of her three-year-old niece, Morgan, who has learned at an early age that Southern women do not hide from encounters with adversity. Morgan had the misfortune of being involved in some mischief at play school. She was disciplined and received a lecture from both teacher and Mom. The next morning on the way to school, her mother sought to underscore the importance of the lecture from the previous day by asking, "Now, Morgan, if someone tries to get you into trouble today, what are you going to do?"

Little Morgan pondered the question quietly with great seriousness before answering in an enthusiastic tone.

"I'm gonna say, 'Wait just a minute and I'll be right there!' "

At three years old, Morgan knows already that Southern women do not run from trouble. We plunge right into it.

There are certain steps we follow in combating adversity. It's a formula that works well for those Southern spitfires who are anything but the weaker sex.

Face it and embrace it—Time spent avoiding an adversarial situation is time spent prolonging it and lengthening or blocking the road to its eventual solution. Time also exacerbates the severity of a problematic situation by allowing it to grow, sometimes beyond control. As my Southern mother often says, "Nip it in the bud." A small bud is much easier to cut off than a massive, overgrown plant. I saw a CEO ousted from a company once after he refused to acknowledge the smattering signs of displeasure from substantial shareholders over a lengthy period of time. By the time he accepted that there was a problem, the situation was well out of control and he found himself no longer in charge.

Prepare for the worst—Preparation is the most effective shield against adversity because it repels many of the poisonous darts that fly in times of trouble. Remember that the worst *seldom,* if *ever,* happens. The very worst I could imagine has never happened to me, although I've wasted a lot of time worrying about it. Instead, think through the problem and prepare mentally and strategically for the worst-case scenario. A real bonus is that once we think the worst, anything else that happens looks much better and is even appreciated. This preparedness allows you to be calm in knowing that nothing will jump into your face for which you are not ready. The key here is to avoid dwelling on the worst because, if you do, you will lose your positive attitude.

Keep a positive mental attitude—Think only positive thoughts. Refuse to succumb to negativity. Manage your mind to keep it from spinning out of control. Our minds and thought processes can be either our strongest ally or most destructive enemy. Choose to make your mental attitude a friend and helpmate by centering yourself with positive thoughts. Granted, this is often the most difficult of all the steps. But, when fighting life's difficulties, it is crucial not to to dwell on past failures but to focus on your successes. During difficult times, your past victories in life are the lifeboat that will keep you afloat. On the other hand, your defeats are a heavy anchor that will weigh you down.

Sometimes it is necessary to segregate yourself from family, friends, or associates who have negative, mealymouthed attitudes. Your attitude—good or bad—is heavily influenced by the company you keep. Stars shine brighter in the reflected glow of other stars.

Be fearless—It's the toughest thing to do in life, but it's the most important if you are to succeed and be happy. Your faith must be stronger than any fear you have. Remind yourself constantly that all things are possible, even the things that do not seem probable. Many people make choices that hamper their happiness because they "fear" what people will think of them if they do not conform to convention. Or, they do not take a risk because they "fear" failure. Or, they do not speak up against injustice because they "fear" retaliation. Safe is not always best. Sometimes, we have to step out of the box of comfort and security that we love and go for the big prize. Do not be afraid to fail because many times we stumble on the way to success. Few successes are gained without the aid of many failures. Henry Ford and Conrad Hilton are just two examples of ultra-successful businesspeople who endured two or more business failures before hitting it big. They were not afraid of failure *or* success.

Control your destiny—When you give in to adversity by throwing up your hands, you have relinquished an important power—that of having a say-so in the outcome of the conflict. The willfulness of Southern women is legendary. We do not let others determine what will happen to our lives without considerable input. We fight, connive, conspire, and sometimes compromise. We do whatever it takes to look after ourselves. When all is said and done, *you* are the only person you can absolutely count on until the day you die. That's not cynicism; it's realism. Those who would protect you might die before you do. So, get used to taking care of yourself! Carefully plan your strategy for overcoming each problem you encounter. Do not handle problems haphazardly, nonchalantly letting come what may. You probably won't like what comes. Instead, steer the solution to your favor.

Move the mountain—We can't always move a mountain that looms in our way with one quick, easy movement from a monstrous piece of equipment like a backhoe. Sometimes mountains have to be removed a shovelful at a time and, to tell you the truth, there have been times I've moved them a teaspoonful at a time. Still, dogged persistence pays off and if you dig long enough, any mountain will eventually disappear from your path. Patience and perseverance are the best tools in the world for moving mountains.

Believe in the good which is there or will come—Every situation has both good and bad attached to it. Sometimes we are so overwhelmed with the magnitude of the bad that we refuse to see any good that is there or will eventually arise from the blackened center of adversity. How many times have you experienced a setback that caused a detour from your normal course, but on that detour you had a glorious blessing dumped in your lap? It happens many times. Don't stare at the doors that close behind you; look ahead toward the wonderful ones that are flung wide open.

I have heard many people express gratitude for the bad times because they showed them who their true friends were. My daddy always said, "Thank God for the hard times because they make the good times taste so much sweeter." As strange as it might seem, none of us would be content and happy if there were no troubling times. We would become bored, and life, at its best, would only be ho-hum.

Those wonderful, exhilarating highs in our life are possible only because we have known the lows. It's very similar to being on a diet, and on this subject I am an absolute expert since I spend at least 50 percent of my days refusing myself epicurean delights—torture in a culture that adores food. Dieting is tough and I hate it, but on the days when I'm not dieting, food is much more delicious and appreciated, particularly when I'm splurging after horrible deprivation. In the unlikely event that I find myself going for a few weeks without having to diet, I become bored with food and, even when I'm hungry, I cannot think of anything I want to eat. That's what life would be like if we only encountered smooth sailing. Tough times increase the succulent flavor and taste of the sweet, happy times.

Learn from the experience—Southern women snatch every opportunity to gain the benefit of knowledge. We love wisdom—partly because we love those opportunities to say "I told you that would happen" when others (others is a secret coded word for "men") are foolish enough to disregard our advice. Adversarial experiences impart to us a wisdom that, if we use it, will enable us to avoid mistakes over and over again.

When we refuse to reflect on the difficult times to discover our errors, we will continue to fall back into the same pit . . . time after time. I decided early on that I made too many first-time mistakes to allow myself the luxury of making the same mistake twice. Why make the same mistake twice when you could be using that time to try a new approach and if you make a new mistake then you'll have an opportunity to gain new wisdom?

Although Southern women sometimes make the same mistakes twice, we preach and practice against it. We try very hard to avoid choosing the wrong kind of man twice. We all make misjudgments about people—particularly in choosing the ones to love and trust. But Southern women don't beat themselves up when they make the wrong choice in love. We just put the blame on him and his upbringing and move on. Then, we make up our minds to choose better and wiser the next time. We do this by examining the mistake and learning from it. As children, we Southern women are taught by our mothers to hold only ourselves responsible for the mistakes we make because we make those choices.

In the South, we do not ostracize people when they make mistakes. Instead, we celebrate the courage it took to take a chance that didn't work out. We applaud the effort and always, without fail, we say, "Well, it could have been worse. Thankfully, it's not worse." Taking it on the chin and moving on makes life less complicated and less stressful.

Keep your problems to yourself—Southern women are very discreet about problems in our relationships and our lives. We may discuss other people's problems, but we never discuss our own outside our families. Many times we do not even discuss our problems within the family. The reasons for our discretion are: First, talking about problems influences the way others think of us and our family. We are a proud host of people for whom family is top priority. Second, once you're willing to forgive an errant husband—for example—you'll find that others never forget and your relationship forever carries a stigma. Third, you never know where or with whom your private information will wind up. Think of discretion as another tactic for controlling your destiny.

In the professional world, problems can be perpetuated by sharing them throughout the office. When conflicts can be handled quickly and quietly, there is no lingering residue or gossip. Not only is discretion a professional courtesy; it also eliminates future resentments and possible conflicts. We have all, at some time, commented on a situation and, as a result, we've created bigger, more embarrassing problems for ourselves.

Confidential information shared with a friend, spouse, or lover could turn into ammunition used by an enemy. Either that confidant, out of the blue, becomes an enemy *or* he naively shares what you've told him with the wrong person. Spouses don't always stay spouses and friends don't always stay friends. Protect yourself wisely and smartly by keeping all loose ends tied up neatly in your own hands. You don't want your secrets to become leverage in someone else's hands, particularly in a labor dispute or divorce case.

Southern women, like all women, are sensitive and emotional. We, too, feel the need to share the secrets of our souls. But we have found ways to do that other than unburdening ourselves to friends over coffee. A Southern woman's top choice for confidante is her mother. Southern mothers are hugely devoted to their children, never condemning and always trustworthy. The second choice is a member of the clergy, therapist, or doctor. They're all bound by ethical guidelines, so enough said.

The best choice, however, is ourselves. Many times, I have had a mirror-to-mirror talk with myself! I sit down at my vanity and talk out my problems. I describe the conflict as if the mirror were another person, and then I articulate my feelings. Gradually, I begin to feel better because I am unburdening my soul and releasing feelings of anxiety. I put myself into the role of the other person and formulate what her suggestions might be for handling the situation. I have solved many problems this way and never run the risk of divulging private information.

In today's world, it is definitely the survival of the fittest where discretion is key to self-protection. Southern women know that and are cunning enough not to give away secrets that could be used against them or theirs.

Don't be a whiner—Strong Southern women do not whine. And, furthermore, we detest it in others. We cannot stomach it, so we refuse to tolerate it. Whiners are weak victims who prefer to whimper about problems rather than solve them. They rely on others to rescue them, and it never occurs to them that they have as much power as anyone has—if they would only tap into it.

Divorces particularly tend to bring out the victim side of women. But not with gutsy, strong Southern women. The moment we realize that divorce is inevitable, we set out to protect and provide for ourselves. We do not whine, beg, or cry. We do not fall to our knees and plead with him to come back. And, we never launch into the poor-me-after-all-I've-done-for-you-and-then-you-dump-me speech. First of all, a confident Southern woman never considers herself "dumped." She considers herself fortunate to be liberated from a loser who doesn't recognize the value of a good woman. Second, it is beneath our dignity to cry and plead. After we are convinced that we have done everything we can to save the marriage, we walk away proudly with our heads held high.

Spunky Southern women do not stay in situations where they are abused emotionally, physically, or mentally. No man is allowed to control us like this even if he has all the money and the house belongs to him. Being a whiner or a victim are not choices for Southern women. We choose to be winners rather than victims.

If you meet a Southern woman who is a whiner, know that she is an outcast, deplored by a sorority on whose proud reputation she has wrought shame and disgrace. Chances are, however, that she isn't a true Southerner. She's probably an immigrant who got sent to the South because the others didn't want her and we were just too gracious to turn her away. Or she might be a first-generation Southerner who hasn't learned proper behavior and protocol yet. In any case, she is definitely a misfit, misplaced in a society of nonwhiners.

I had the ulcer-producing experience of working with a classic whiner once in an office filled with strong, noncomplaining Southern women. The whiner was intellectually bright, but emotionally challenged. She whined and complained about *everything.* At first, we were patient, even kind and consoling. Eventually, though, we became intolerant and scornfully mocking. Our covert distaste turned to overt disdain. She became an ugly pimple on the beautiful complexion of our office.

She was also an insidious manipulator who used her whining to get out of tasks she determined to be undesirable or beneath her. Southern women never, ever consider themselves to be "above" honest work of any kind. We jump in and do whatever needs doing without complaint or comment.

The best thing I can say about that young woman is that she was not bred or raised as a Southern lady, for I would hate to know that the South had produced such a sorry example of womanhood. This was painfully apparent when she joked repeatedly and irreverently about our hallowed tradition of serving deviled eggs at all family gatherings.

That was the straw that broke the camel's back.

Impostors aside, Southern women will first always try graciousness and diplomacy to smooth a situation and settle conflicts. If that doesn't work after repeated tries, we just get downright mean. That's when the devil meets his match!

CHAPTER FOURTEEN

Choose Your Battles Carefully:

If Custer Had, He Wouldn't Be Buried in the Middle of Nowhere

Although Southern women never shrink from confrontation, they know that battles chosen carefully are battles more easily won. Southern women strongly advocate winning through strategic shrewdness rather than combat. For that reason, our full-fledged battles are few and far between. In fact, an all-out war is always our last resort and used *only* when everything else has failed and the issue at hand is of vital importance.

Properly trained Southern women always choose disarming charm over angry words, innuendoes, and ultimatums. Not only is beguiling charm less stressful for all involved; it also prevents the inevitable bitterness that rises from the ashes of battle. A win at all costs is often too expensive in the long run.

Whether you're at the office or home, remind yourself that everything is not worth the high cost of combat. Period. In fact, few things are worth the emotional price extracted either from a small battle or an ongoing war. Petty arguments turn into battles and battles into war. That is how marriages fall apart and professional relationships disintegrate. In the end, after months or years of on-again, off-again war, the initial cause can usually be traced back to something as simple as an argument over who last took out the trash or a clash over who should make the coffee at the office. Every argument, regardless of how minor, breaks away a tiny chip from the foundation of a relationship.

For that reason, it is gloriously beneficial to charm rather than harm.

Bite your tongue quickly. Choke down angry words. Make noncommittal statements that do not betray ugly feelings. You want to leave the door open to come back and present your case when your thoughts are completely rational.

Take the necessary time to regroup. Carefully think about the situation and plot your strategy. Decide *what* you want and then determine *how* you will get it.

Use your woman's intuition. It's your best ally because it will always guide you to the best solution. Do what your gut instinct says. A strong intuition is better than logic or a high I.Q. Instinctively, we know when to keep our mouths shut. Too many times we don't listen to that instinct, only to regret it later.

Learn to read people carefully. Know which buttons to push and when. Realize that people are as unique as each set of fingerprints. The same approach will not work on every person or in every situation. Tailor the approach to the person and the situation.

Prepare yourself to argue with reason, not emotion. Arguments are won more quickly with reasonable words and persuasion than with irrational emotion.

Do your homework. Collect all the data and analytical information that supports your argument. In other words, don't argue emptily with nothing other than emotion to support your point.

Aim for a satisfying compromise. Don't be selfish. Find a solution that works well for everyone. Remember: Southern women always work toward a "win-win" situation.

Behave in a detached manner. Smile charmingly and do not let anger enter your voice. Never let your tone stray past firmness and confidence.

Approach the opponent in a positive manner. Build up the ego of your opposition rather than tearing it down. Make sure the opponent feels like an important part of the solution.

Charmingly plead your case, repeatedly and relentlessly. The use of charm often takes longer than the abrasive tactics that beat a person quickly and bitterly into retreat. Charm is like pouring muriatic acid on concrete. It takes longer, but it does a beautiful job of dissolving stubborn, built-up resistance.

Fight only when absolutely necessary. When all else fails—and this is truly important—launch into full battle when you finally attack. If you rarely, if ever, fight, you will have the advantage of catching the opposition off guard. A surprise attack on an unsuspecting opponent means almost certain victory.

Ready. Aim. Fire. Once you launch a fight, be prepared to fight with everything possible and never consider the possibility of defeat. If you lose, life is going to be much less pleasant, once you've taken this big jump.

Don't be too proud to make the right decision for you. If the issue at hand is not important, then shrug it off and move on. Protect your emotional health and your relationships by calling an immediate truce. But turn this to your advantage, by proving what a good sport you are. Tell your colleague, "Okay, you win. I would prefer it another way, but I'm a team player and I'll support you to the best of my ability." Say to your husband, "Honey, I love you and if it's that important to you to take the job transfer, I will do my best to make it as easy as possible for the entire family." When you handle a situation this way, you have still won the war even if you lost the battle.

We Southern women are great fighters, but we do it so charmingly that no one suspects how hard we are fighting. Sometimes we win by pretending to give up. This is just a commando tactic, though, because we are waiting for the appropriate time to pick up our weapons and start over again. As I told you—we're relentless and willful. Southern wives usually win by using copious amounts of energy to wear down their husbands. Of course, the husbands always think the solution was their idea—a thought heartily and shrewdly endorsed by the wives.

Southern women reduce stress and aggravation by carefully choosing which battles to fight and which ones aren't worth the emotional ammunition required to slay the beast. Remember Scarlett's "I'll think about that tomorrow"? That is typical of most Southern women. We don't ignore problems or conflicts, but we are wise enough to know that the passing of time settles many things without our assistance. If time doesn't resolve the problem, we grab our armor and plunge into battle.

Life is too short to worry needlessly. Sometimes, the most effective defense is no defense. In other words, just sit back for a little while and let a situation work out its own kinks. This is similar to the natural healing of a wound when the skin grows back together. In short, don't worry excessively about a problem until it proves itself worthy of your concern.

Smart Southern women avoid unnecessary and excessive confrontation in the workplace. It is rare to find a Southern woman who is constantly argumentative and difficult on the job. First of all, her manners prevent such behavior. Second, she correctly realizes that she will be labeled as a "bitch" or malcontent, which will decrease her effectiveness. She rarely argues with her male colleagues. She charms them, instead. She works *with* them and never *against* them. Not only does sweet honey attract bears; a sweet approach also eliminates the unnecessary tension associated with bitchiness.

I once worked with a non-Southern woman who both looked and acted like a monster. She was nasty and hateful, and practically everyone throughout the company despised her. She waged full-fledged war against anyone who crossed her for the most minor of reasons. It was rumored that she had a "hit list" and disposed of her enemies one by one. If winning required complete annihilation of an enemy, then she did it. As a result, she was labeled a classic bitch and shunned by everyone whenever possible. No one wanted to work with her, so we often worked around her. Sadly, she had a brilliant mind, but she chose to use it in a destructive rather than constructive manner. Because she created extreme stress for herself during her tirades, she was regularly sick with stomach and digestive problems—an unattractive problem for an unattractive person.

Although conquering through charm sounds easier said than done, it is much easier than other argumentative ways. To illustrate this concept, let's look at two different ways of handling the same situation.

Scenario: A woman is called in for a meeting with her boss, in which he announces a decision that she vehemently opposes. He plans to move her best-performing employee to another department because the company would benefit greatly from the move. The female manager is well respected by her boss and is free to speak her mind on the subject.

Likely female reaction. Anger visibly crosses her face, eyes flashing darkly, she throws her hand on her hips and leans forward and sneers, "You're not really going to do *that*, are you?" The boss immediately becomes defensive, not because she has overstepped the bounds but because she has insinuated that he is an idiot. He pulls back in his chair and stares at her for a moment before his defensiveness flashes into play.

A battle of some proportion ensues. As the heat of the verbal exchanges accelerate, the damage deepens. The discussion may end there, but, more than likely, it will stretch on for days and with each passing day will become more destructive to the working relationship. More than likely, this woman will not win because she came out of the corner swinging wildly. And, in the bargain, she causes severe damage to her working relationship with her boss that may never be totally repaired.

Southern version: A Southern woman reacts by choking down the words of anger that want to leap from her lips. Instead, she pauses for a moment, gathers her thoughts, and then reacts with amused surprise. She lowers her chin slightly, glancing upward through her lashes at her boss—male or female. She smiles sweetly, understandingly, and then laughs lightly.

"You're not really going to do that, *are you?*" The same words with a different inflection. She uses a tone that is light and nonaccusing, yet it expresses the same thought as the previous woman—she is not pleased with the decision or in agreement with it. Her laughter makes the idea sound so ludicrous that the other person immediately doubts himself. This creates a window of opportunity for persuading a change of mind.

It only takes a moment for her to realize that she is up to bat with the bases loaded and two outs in the bottom of the ninth. Not the best of situations. She begins to plead her case charmingly. She keeps her tone light and friendly, never angry. She starts by building up the ego of her boss.

"You're one of the smartest people I know," she reasons. "I have great faith in your ability to make the right decision. And, I know that you'll make the right decision because you always do."

Her boss smiles. He is charmingly disarmed. She swings at the first pitch as it comes straight across the plate plainly in the strike zone.

"Is this change absolutely set in stone?"

"Well, no, but almost," he hedges. Her bat now connects with the ball, producing a good, solid hit.

"Will you allow me to give you some insight that I am sure you have already considered, but will make me feel better to say it?"

"Of course," he agrees.

Because she has not gotten riled up to the point of irrational thinking, she is able to challenge the decision with reason, not emotion. On the other hand, the first woman continues in a fit by saying, "I can't believe you're going to do this. It makes no sense. It is absolutely stupid (which is the same as saying the other person is stupid). The first woman is sinking further in the mud while the second boss is throwing down planks over the mud holes for the Southern woman to cross.

The Southern woman wraps up her presentation and then says, "I just ask that you reconsider it after the things I have said. Meanwhile, I'd like to have a few days to think of an alternative solution."

He agrees, and she prepares to leave his office. Just before she steps out the door, she turns around, wags her finger playfully, and says with a big, bright smile in a teasing tone, "Now, remember I *know* you'll make the right decision. Just don't forget what the right decision is!"

That hit eventually turns into a game-winning grand-slam home run.

Sometimes in situations like this, we exaggerate our charm and make the situation playfully funny. Either way, it works the same because a frivolous tone puts others in a lighthearted frame of mind that works much better when straightening out differences. Handling situations in this manner is fun, not stressful. It is productive, not destructive.

While Southern women extol charm as the most effective weapon for slaying giants, bosses, and husbands, we never allow ourselves to be punching bags. So when all else fails, we come out throwing our white-gloved punches. Since we choose our battles carefully and fight rarely, the opponent isn't expecting the transformation of the lovely gardenia bush into a briar patch filled with poisonous berries. Without fail, the recipient of these blows falls stunned to his knees. He never sees the punch coming, proving that a surprise attack is always a winner.

If you have worked in a company for a period of time, during which you used charm and civility to negotiate through problem situations, no one will ever suspect the demon you can be when backed into a corner. This secret is so much to your advantage, you won't believe it. Remember the Japanese surprise attack on Pearl Harbor in 1941? Not only did the Japanese choose the early dawn when many were still asleep; they also chose Sunday, a quiet day of rest and relaxation. Their chances for success were much higher than they would have been on a weekday afternoon when the base was on full alert.

Make your choices carefully when you launch a surprise attack. Consider that you have one good chance, and then go for it. Once you make up your mind to fight, do what any Southern woman worth her grits does—fight with all your might and don't give up until you win or you ruin your manicure, whichever comes first.

Be cautious about jumping into the ring with a male colleague, however, because men and women fight differently. When women fight, whether it's with men or women, they don't forget. Ever. This means the women eventually wind up with resentment.

On the other hand, men fight differently against women than they do other men. When men disagree or do battle among themselves, they forget it when it's over and move on. Therefore, those relationships are seldom damaged. But when businessmen fight with women, neither party forgets. Men resent being locked in battle with women because it is an uncomfortable, nonchivalrous, unnatural position to be in. Tensions and bitterness build and relationships become permanently damaged.

That's why it's best to charm 'em, win the battle like a lady, and keep everyone friendly.

You are the only person who can decide if the situation is worth the fight or if it's better to drop it and move on to something else. But as any Southerner knows, if you get knocked down in a battle, get back up, and fight again and keep fighting until you win.

My brother-in-law shared a true story with me about a young man he knows who was a terrible nuisance on the school bus when he was youngster. Every morning and every afternoon, the nine-year-old was in a fight on the bus. Finally, one day the school-bus driver had enough of the rowdy behavior, so he pulled the bus over to the side of the road and stopped.

"Jimmy, come here," he demanded, wiggling his finger. "You and me need to have a talk."

With head down and lips pursed, Jimmy made his way to the front of the bus.

"This fighting has got to stop," the bus driver said sternly. "Every morning and every afternoon, you're in a fight. I can't have it anymore. It has to stop."

Jimmy jerked his head up and looked at the school-bus driver with heartbreak in his eyes. With the greatest desperation possible in his voice, he pleaded, "But, Mr. Jackson, you don't understand! One day, *I'm* going to win!"

At nine years old, that young boy knew what it took me three decades to learn—that if we fight long enough and hard enough, we *will* win. However, if it had been a Southern girl rather than a boy, she would have known that she didn't have to fight twice a day, every day, to eventually find victory. She would have chosen her battles more carefully and won more quickly. Probably the first time.

CHAPTER FIFTEEN

When Love Doesn't Treat You Like a Lady, Teach It Better Manners

LOVE AND ROMANCE healthily thrive in the South. We are, without a doubt, the most romantic culture in the United States. We love starry nights dreamily spent on the veranda swing or in the gazebo. We adore romantic clothing, particularly lovely lingerie. We practice the art of being the perfect girlish woman—that intoxicating blend of childish innocence, womanly worldliness, and sexiness.

We work hard to make relationships fulfilling and as perfect as possible. We concentrate on putting our best foot and best face forward. Many Southern women care more about how they look after they marry than they did before they landed a husband. No truer words were ever spoken than those by my sister, who has been successfully married to her only husband for over twenty-five years, "It's a lot easier to get a husband than to *keep* one." *Touché.*

When love does not treat a Southern woman like a lady, the next time she grabs it by the ears and sets about teaching it better manners. When a relationship ends, we learn from it, rather than burn over it. We review our own mistakes and evaluate how to correct them. We know that until a lesson is firmly learned, we will keep making the same mistakes over and over. We then decide what we want and don't want from a man in our next relationship. We do not waste our time or expend any energy by choosing the very same kind of man again. So, learn from your mistake the first time and get on with your love life.

Work hard, though, to prevent a breakup before it can happen. Indulge in romantic love—flickering fires, baths lighted by candlelight and decorated with rose petals, scented bedsheets that have been sprayed with perfume and powdered, picnics under a full moon and stars. Use your femininity in full force, because it is your greatest asset. Southern women primp, pamper, and preen since we want to keep his attentions directed toward us and away from another alluring vixen.

Always wear beautiful lingerie even under business suits. If you feel beautiful and sexy, you'll act that way. Gorgeous lingerie gives you that little extra oomph that will separate you from the women who wear full, white cotton briefs. You can tell by carefully observing a woman what type of lingerie she is wearing. Very often, my lingerie is more beautiful than the clothes I am wearing. The next time you're at a party, look around the room and play a game of trying to figure out who's wearing what. Very quickly, you'll discover that women who are prancing around as though they're a reincarnation of Venus, goddess of love, have an extra secret hidden somewhere. Usually, it's under their clothes in the form of lace, silk, or satin that makes them act coquettish. Believe me, men greatly appreciate this attention to detail. And, don't scoff at the notion by whimpering that it's uncomfortable. Adjust, adapt, and reap the benefits. A realtor's slogan may be "Location! Location! Location!" But, a Southern woman's motto is "Details! Details! Details!" Always remember that the details are the extra advantage that every woman wants and needs.

Be the perfect girlish woman—an irresistible blend of wide-eyed wonder, worldliness, and sexiness. Do not allow yourself to become matronly with age by wearing severely cut clothes and a chopped-off, blunt, unstylish hairdo. Keep your look updated and fresh. A hard-edged woman who thinks she has all the answers is a turnoff to men because they need to feel that they have something to contribute to the relationship. Many Southern women have as much girlish charm at eighty as they had at eighteen. My mother, who is in her seventies, does. She giggles, flirts, and entices. She does so in a well-mannered way, of course. But she does it.

Love what he loves. Find out what is important to him and make it important to you. If he loves pro wrestling (gulp), learn to love it or, at least, tolerate it. Enjoy and share with him and you will find that he responds most favorably to such treatment. It is important to give every relationship all you have so that if it ends, you will have no regrets about what you did not do. A lack of such regrets makes it easier to heal and move on.

Make yourself indispensable, but don't smother him. Give him his freedom to come and go, but when he is there, make his life easier and more comfortable. A good and decent Southern woman never balks when her man asks for a bowl of ice cream after she sits down to enjoy a movie with him. She'll never say, "Get it yourself." The worst she will ever venture to say is, "Okay, honey. If you'll wait a moment until a commercial comes on, I'll be happy to get it for you."

Don't let a bad day turn into a week, then into a month, then a year, and finally forever. We all have mornings when we crawl out of bed with a surly, cat-on-a-hot-tin-roof feeling. Those are the days when everything rubs us the wrong way. Fine. That's understandable. But don't let that day be followed by another so that you act unattractively for two days in a row. A series of days like that signal habit, and that kind of habit pushes a man out the door. When you have a bad day, apologize and make it up to him in a special way.

What's in a name? Southern women don't hyphenate maiden names with married names. We love the men we marry and are honored to take their names. This is a small concession that reaps many benefits. To us, it signifies that we are a unit, a package that coexists to complement each other's strengths. Men are lovingly more willing to accept us as equal, intelligent partners because their egos are soothed and they don't feel they are involved in a power struggle. As you know, power struggles—real or imagined—cause people to work against each other, not together. A healthy marriage requires working together. If a man tells you that he is comfortable with a hyphenated marriage name, don't believe it. Deep down, his male ego will resent it, and that sore will continue to fester until it erupts into other problems.

Women in the South—particularly career women—will often use both names after a marriage for a period of time. Jane Connor becomes Jane Connor Black. However, the second name will frequently disappear after business associates have acclimated to the woman's marriage name. Now, that's okay to do. It is also all right if she is extremely well known professionally, if she continues to use that name as long as she only uses it in her career and doesn't expect her children to carry it. But that hyphen. *That* hyphen. Oh, the unnecessary problems wrought by such decisions! We know that our personal identity is tied to much more than a name. It is tied to our personal and professional accomplishments.

Incidentally, in many higher-society circles of the South, women identify themselves by their husbands' names, such as Mrs. Richard Blake. A few years ago, I purchased a Junior League cookbook (those Junior Leaguers really know how to cook) in a gift shop in Asheville, North Carolina. At the end of each recipe was the name of the member who submitted it. The names were listed either as Mrs. Carl Moses or Mary Carsten Moses (Mrs. Carl).

What can I say? Tradition dies hard in the South, but mainly because we refuse to kill it.

The best way to keep a man is to let him go. It's important to allow him the freedom to move about without a hawk eye following his every movement. No one—male or female—is comfortable with constant surveillance. Only women with low self-confidence throw jealous fits and check up on their companions without reason. If a man throws enough evidence in your face, don't be a fool—find out what's going on. If there's no reason to suspect, though, don't inspect! Women, who have done everything to make themselves appealing are confident enough to know their men will always come back. These women do not worry or fret.

"Kindness and sugar will get you everything," drawls my friend Virgie. "You have to have a willingness to make him special."

It is also Virgie who contends that a man and his mind can be changed by employing a Southern woman's charms. "There's only one woman who can change a man and his mind. And, she ain't born in New York." But Virgie doesn't hesitate to add, "Of course, if she's willing to learn from us, she could charm the rattlers off a snake!"

Spoil him. It may sound old-fashioned, but I know a lot of women who would like to go back to the old-fashioned times when marriages lasted fifty and sixty years. How do you think that happened? Because women knew how to make themselves an indispensable part of their men's lives. Indispensable means you can't do without someone, so divorce is out of the question. My mom and dad were married for fifty-eight years until he passed away, and every day of those fifty-eight years, my mother took his supper to him on a tray and woke him with a cup of coffee in bed.

Cook his favorite foods, wash his favorite shirt with care, surprise him with that CD or book he wanted. Surprise him at the airport when he returns from a business trip. Tuck a love note into his pocket or a sweet card into his briefcase. Make him feel that he is special and cherished.

When he says "How can I ever thank you for all your thoughtfulness?" lower your chin shyly, look up through mascara-coated lashes, and murmur softly, "All I ever want is just to be adored by you." It works like a charm, every time. You will be surprised how quickly men begin to parrot the words you teach them by saying, "I just adore you, do you know that?" Men express what they are taught in a relationship, and there are so many more interesting words than *love* or *honey.*

We Southern women train our men early in a new relationship to call us "precious," "baby," "sweetheart," and other endearing niceties. How? Very simply, we lead by example. We begin by calling our man by all those endearing names and, eventually, he decides that it sounds so good that those words begin to tumble effortlessly off his tongue. Before he realizes it, he will be mimicking the same sweet words that you use.

Love deeply—but not with all your heart. Southern women are cunning enough to handle relationships more from the mind than from the heart. This enables us to maintain more control over the course of the relationship than if we follow our hearts exclusively. This completely baffles men because they see total devotion, sensuality, and fluttery charm, yet the woman doesn't grovel. When there is an argument, she doesn't beg for forgiveness, call repeatedly, or drive by his house. If he is wrong, she waits for an apology. If she is wrong, she doesn't hesitate to apologize but she does so in a responsible, adult manner. She never pleads. Because Southern women deal more analytically than emotionally, we see and accept when we are wrong. We do not hesitate to apologize (but always in a straightforward, nongroveling manner). We do not believe that the man is always wrong—just sometimes.

Let bygones be bygones. This is a Southern way of saying we know better than to hold a grudge or to repeatedly bring up mistakes that happened years ago. It is counterproductive, negative, and, in the long run, detains us from getting things we want—we're always smart enough to look out for what is in our best long-term interest. It is important always to focus on what lies down the road and not what is right in your face at the moment. If you remember that, you'll be more successful in getting the things that are truly important. Plus, you'll have more peace and contentment.

If you persist in beating up on a man mentally and emotionally, you are your own worst enemy. His resentment builds and it eventually destroys the relationship. The biggest danger is that he will start looking for someone else. Sometimes for comfort and many times to show that he has real power in the relationship—the power to hurt you and to do things that you can't control. Besides—and this is the most critical thing to remember—when a man is emotionally embattled, he is distracted from thinking of the flowers he wants to send, the jewelry he wants to buy, the surprise vacation he wants to give you. Help him keep his mind clear so that he can do wonderful things for you!

Lisa, one of my best friends since junior high, endured the hardship of a failed first marriage but made a sensational match the second time around with a special man. She remarried well, lives in a spectacular house, drives a zippy foreign car, and would never have to work a day in her life, *if* she chose. Yet, she works to create an identity for herself and to make her own niche in the world. Several years ago, she bought a darling gift store, and now she devotes tireless energy to this successful venture. I am so proud of her. But I am especially proud when she calls while luxuriating in a hot bubble bath at the end of a busy day. Without fail, the call always ends with some slight variation of:

"Oh, I have to go. Dan just came in here to tell me that he has dinner prepared. So I need to get out of the tub and dry off. I'll talk to you later."

Sound like a fairy tale? Not hardly. She works hard at the store *and* at home. Dan never feels that he comes second. He knows he comes first in her life and, as a result, he heaps attention and affection on her. And although he works extremely hard each day, he comes home every evening and cooks a wonderful dinner. Every woman should be as lucky . . . or at least as *smart* as Lisa. She is independent, but not so much so that her husband feels unneeded or unimportant.

Life is never perfect, though. So when love fails us, we pick up the pieces and move on without bitterness or vengeance. We learn from our mistakes and dwell on the happy moments of those relationships rather than the bad times. Our dramatic mothers (Southern women *love* drama) never fail to remind us that "it is better to have loved and lost than never to have loved at all." With happiness, however, eventually comes pain of some kind.

Above all, we never stop believing in love and romance, whether love disappoints us or rewards us. We Southern women do not believe that a man is necessary to complete our being, but rather to enhance it. We do not lose our identity in our man's identity. In fact, we cling furiously and tenaciously to our own. In the South, you will find that even women who marry extremely well and do not desire a career proudly create and mold their own identities through civic and volunteer efforts. They are never simply "Mrs." Anybody. They are individuals who make significant contributions to society. Besides, intermingling identities and losing yourself completely in your husband's identity makes it harder to walk away from marriage if that becomes necessary. And, we Southern women do not allow love or a loveless marriage to control us and our destinies.

Savvy Southern women appreciate and cherish a loving relationship and work hard to preserve it. We never treat the men in our lives as dispensable or replaceable. We treat them as precious, devoted partners. Yet when a strong Southern woman does not have a romantic involvement, she doesn't flit the days away by whining, crying, and feeling sorry for herself. She makes the most of life by enjoying her time alone and being productive with activities that enhance her life personally or professionally. It is unproductive to mope around, tearfully wishing for Prince Charming to come riding up on his white stallion. Know that, in time, he *will* come. He always does. Meanwhile, enjoy life to the fullest. You can never get back the time that you throw away.

It is unfortunate that all relationships do not work out, so it is just as critical to know how to handle a breakup successfully as it is to know how to handle a healthy relationship. When a relationship ends, smart Southern women accept the fact gracefully and without bitterness. We do not treat him harshly or unfairly and talk unkindly about him with our friends. This, too, is counterproductive behavior because it perpetuates the sadness within us and causes the problem to linger longer with everyone—especially between the two of you.

We Southern women strongly believe that publicly belittling the men we once loved is a disgraceful commentary on our own judgment and choices. After all, a woman who ends a relationship is the same woman who *chose* that man in the first place. I have made some foolish (that's a nice word for *stupid*) choices in men, but I had more pride and sense than to broadcast to the world what an idiot I was. When someone tries to delve into why the relationship ended, say no more than "He's a wonderful person, but, unfortunately, things don't always work out—even between *two* wonderful people." Then, change the subject. Smart Southern women *never* admit they were wrong about a man.

A huge benefit of such admirable behavior is the effect it has on potential suitors. Since every woman has her own particular social circle, more often than not, her next suitor will come from that circle either as the gentleman caller himself or through an introduction. Because we don't talk bitterly and vindictively about our exes, other men are more immediately attracted to us. After all, who wants to risk a relationship with a woman who is going to rip him to shreds later if it doesn't work out? Do you think that a man would want to marry a woman whom he watched annihilate her last husband in a bitter divorce? Not unless he's stupid and can't find any other woman to marry. Which, by the way, is not the case in some cities where women are said to outnumber the men two to one! With those kinds of odds, you simply must be on your best behavior! The bottom line is that men with class appreciate women who act with class.

I will always be inspired by my friend Martie and how she once handled a long-term relationship that ended. She was very much in love with the guy and had serious thoughts of marriage. Since we worked together, she often mentioned him in passing during day-to-day conversation. One day, it occurred to me that she had not mentioned him recently.

Thinking nothing of it, I asked, "How's John doing?"

As if it were yesterday, I can still see her as she continued to sift through papers on her desk. She shrugged slightly, but a tortured look of sadness and heartbreak shrouded her face. "I don't know. We broke up three weeks ago." Her lip quivered very slightly, but she smiled sweetly.

Imagine that! Her world had crumbled weeks before, but she kept up a stoic appearance, never missed a day of work, and carried on with great courage.

My heart hurt for my dear friend. "You broke up three weeks ago and you never mentioned it?"

"No." She smiled tightly again and shook her head. I rushed over to her, so amazed by the dignity with which she had conducted herself. I threw my arms around her and exclaimed—she laughs today about this—"Oh, my dear, sweet Martie. What a brave little soldier you have been!"

I meant it, though. Her classy way of handling such a difficult breakup has been a constant inspiration to me over the years. What man in his right mind wouldn't want a woman with the kind of class that Martie possesses? And, of course, that kind of class landed her a wonderful husband, beautiful children, and a lovely house in the suburbs.

I have known Southern women who, with the calmest demeanor possible, endured the most atrocious behavior by their husbands. You will find this mostly in the more rural areas of the South where bad behavior by men tends to be overlooked more sweepingly by long-suffering, noncomplaining wives. Southern women in the more populated areas are not as generous or, perhaps, as blatantly blind.

I remember hearing my grandmother tell stories from time to time of men "who would lay up drunk for a week and wouldn't even strike a lick at a rattlesnake if it was fixin' to bite." Or the ones who "went off ever Saturdee night with some floozy he picked up in the roadhouse." And, of course, these men were always married to women with hearts of gold who had birthed at least a dozen children. I often wondered how women could put up with such behavior until I heard one such martyr say, "Whatcha gotta remember is he's basically a good man with a good heart. He jest makes some bad decisions from time to time. That's all."

From that woman I learned that we see what we want to see in people. While everyone else saw all the bad in her man, she chose to find the good and to dwell on that. Or, maybe like other Southern women, she just didn't want to admit she had made a mistake!

Handle yourself with grace and dignity and behave like a lady. Particularly if you want him back. If you make a ladylike exit, you will find that he *always* comes back—even if it's years later and you no longer want him. The key is to allow the hurt to settle down and then, many months later, pick up a friendship. Offer your friendship and mean it. Then, be there for him when he needs a friend. I can say unequivocally that this has worked for me every time.

Every man who has ever been important to me romantically is still a wonderful friend, including my ex-husband. Why would you share the most intimate parts of your life and soul with someone and then write him off as a complete stranger? Especially when he knows you better than even your best girlfriend or mother? If you ruthlessly cut someone like that from your life, you have sliced away a precious piece of your heart and tossed it away. The only exception to this would be in the case of physical abuse, for which there is absolutely no excuse. The rules have been broken by a man who abuses you and you should never—ever, under any circumstances—associate with him again. Never give up your power to a villain like that.

After years of trial and error, I have discovered the best way to achieve this special friendship. The most important step is to part ways in a civil manner. Breaking up is not the time for unburdening your soul of each resentment you harbor or every slight you've endured in the relationship. Those things should have been aired at the time of their occurrence and then tossed away. Do not tell him how horrible and despicable he is. Tell him instead how nice he is and remind him of all the wonderful qualities he has. Remember: You chose him and fell in love with him, so there are some nice things there that attracted you. Then, leave it at that and walk away.

Later, that insidious beast of anger will, more than likely, claw at your heart and torment your mind. Those feelings will make you yearn to pick up the phone and give him a piece of your mind. DON'T. Your state of mind is temporary, so get away from that telephone and stay away from it until the feeling passes. It will. Don't undo the good you have done by saying words that can't be unsaid and will always be remembered.

Think of yourself as a magnanimous, wonderful individual who is well-bred and who always takes the high road. Believe me, when you handle a difficult breakup this way, your roads will always intersect again.

With that done, the next step is to give it time. The old adage "time heals" is true because time creates distance and distance dulls emotion. After a certain period, which could range from months to years, you'll find you don't think so unkindly of him. The good memories will surface far more often and with greater intensity than the bad ones. When that time arrives, give him a call or send a short note and say, "I just want to thank you for being an important part of my life. I'm sorry that it didn't work out, but at least we had some happy times together and I'm grateful for those. If I can ever help you in any way, please do not hesitate to call." It is a lovely gesture, and it will always offer its rewards—if nothing more than giving *you* peace and tranquillity about the relationship.

One thing is certain when employing this method: he will always be a friend who can be counted on, and a big piece of his heart will always belong to such a terrific woman. This also paves the way for telephoning later to ask for big favors. I only hope you were smart enough to choose a man in the first place who's capable of rendering important favors! If not, you need to work on that piece of shortsightedness.

When we Southern women choose the next man, we refuse to judge the new man in our lives by men from the past. If your former paramour was a habitual liar (I could really share some stories on that one), do not allow that fact to place doubt in your new relationship. Yes, of course, you'll be more cautious, but do not jeopardize a new relationship by dragging in ghosts from your past. Some women think they can use it as an excuse. Absolutely not. Making him suffer for past men in your life is inexcusable behavior and is not fair to the innocent man who had the misfortune of following the disreputable scoundrel into your life.

One day, I ran into a casual acquaintance and his new girlfriend at the gym. He introduced us. I spoke to her for a moment and then went on to do my workout. He and I ended up on equipment close together, and we chatted for a few minutes while exercising. Suddenly, she stormed over, told him she was leaving and she would see him later. She bolted toward the exit, but he grabbed her and suddenly a war of words erupted. When she left, I sauntered over, rather amused by the tasteless display (proper Southern women never create scenes in public) and asked casually, "Was that little scene about me?"

He looked sheepish and nodded.

"Why would you put up with something like that?" I asked. "We did not talk for more than three or four minutes."

"Her ex-husband really did a number on her emotionally," he explained. "He ran around on her and lied to her. Now, she's very insecure, and it causes a lot of trouble in our relationship."

Think that relationship lasted? Let's put it this way: You could count on fewer than two hands the number of months that it survived. In short, don't bring baggage from past relationships into new ones. Get over it or get counseling, but don't sabotage a new relationship.

A true, well-bred Southern woman never utters the words "That's a man for you!" Such general, sweeping statements are in poor taste, untrue, and they become another of those stumbling blocks that slow us down en route to getting what we want and desire in life. Judge every man on his own merits—or lack of them.

The bottom line is that when love treats us badly, we Southern women do not run and hide from it the next time around. We simply work harder the next time around. When one relationship ends, we always walk away like a lady with our heads held high and our high heels clicking just as fast as they'll go!

CHAPTER SIXTEEN

We'd Rather Have a Broken Heart Than a Broken Set of China

The women of the South know how to repair broken hearts, but a broken set of china is a heartbreak that can't be fixed. What it boils down to is, we don't mind what breaks as long as it's something we can fix or, at least, replace.

In the early, formative years of our Southern womanhood, we tend to get our hearts broken a great deal because we're dewy-eyed with untainted sensitivity and romance. During that time, we gain valuable experience in heartbreak first aid. Then, we wise up and learn how to enjoy romance without giving our hearts completely and totally. Yet, those early years provide important training for us, and what we learn is this: Men are easier to replace than a broken set of grandmother's china.

In the South, there has yet to be found a man who could come between a woman and her family china. We take heirlooms very seriously. We know that it is easy to hide a mended, tattered heart but a broken china plate is another matter altogether and one that should not be regarded with any degree of frivolity. As my friend Deb says, "My heart's been broken so many times that it's impossible to break it anymore."

A few years ago, during a physical examination, a doctor listened to my heart several times and then shook his head.

"You have a little bit of an irregular heartbeat, and that concerns me." He was slightly annoyed when I shrugged nonchalantly.

"Young lady, this could be serious," he lectured sternly.

I waved away his concern. "Don't worry about it. Look, you'd have an irregular heartbeat, too, if your heart had been broken as many times as mine has!"

Southern women are good sports about the loss of love—mainly, because we rarely view it as a failure on our part. We do everything we can possibly do to make it work and then, if it doesn't, we have no regrets or remorse. My grandmother always said there's someone for everyone. And, as an example, she always used her childhood friend Buella Mae Potter who was, as the old folks like to say, "a bit touched in the head" but who found lasting love with Roy Boy Henry, the survivor of an accident in which a mighty oak limb had fallen on his head when he was a child.

"Nary a week goes by that I don't think of them two. Happy as two pigs in a poke, they was," she would recall. "Betwixt them, they didn't have as much common sense as a child. So, you can only reckon as to how they managed. But somehow they got along mightily and they couldn't have been more content if they'd been the king and queen of England. Always holdin' hands and actin' silly over each other. That right there showed me that God's got someone for everyone."

Today's Southern women, however, realize that it's even

better than what grandmother thought. Not only is there someone for everyone; there's *at least* two or three others who will work just as well. When a relationship or marriage ends, we know—in fact we're confident—that another wonderful someone will come along. We never waste time dwelling on what is lost. Instead, we turn our energy to the future and excitedly anticipate the next prince who will roar onto the scene in his jazzy sports car.

When a relationship ends, we do not wring our hands and fretfully cry, "Why, oh why did I get involved with him?" We know that each man and every relationship has an important purpose in our lives—sometimes it is to teach us things about life; other times, it is to teach us things about ourselves. But whatever it is, we know it is an important lesson that we can't afford to miss. Nor, would we want to. We are undaunted by anguish that was preceded by loads of funs and tons of kisses.

We do not allow a breakup to undermine our self-confidence. Realistically, we realize that all personalities and lifestyles do not mix and nothing is wrong with us if a man chooses another. When you think about it, there are many things that have to blend to make a harmonic relationship—two people must have the same basic philosophies about family, children, life, work, and religion. They must also possess the same basic energy levels (a lazy person will never survive with a nonstop go-getter), similar likes and dislikes, compatible educational or success levels, and emotional synergy (a sensitive person does not mesh with an uncompassionate type).

Then, of course, great importance is placed on the physical attraction—and that is something that definitely cannot be manufactured. It comes naturally, and either you have it or you don't. I have dated handsome, wonderful men who fit the bill perfectly except that their kisses did not give me goose bumps. Without goose bumps, a relationship is doomed. Period. I, like many women, have said from time to time, "He's gorgeous. He's wonderful. He's successful. In fact, he's perfect. So, what's wrong with me?" The answer is "nothing," other than that Venus, the goddess of love and desire, chose not, for whatever reason, to sprinkle her magical, passionate dust on that particular union.

As for me, I never take it personally when a man is not attracted to me because I know that physical attraction is not confined strictly to beauty or sexiness. It is simply a complicated, chemical reaction that we do not and cannot control.

Southern mothers, as they prepare their daughters for the arduous task of finding a husband, always pound two bits of very good advice into our heads:

Don't ever go out on a first date with someone to whom you can't imagine yourself married. How true. We've all been guilty at one time or other of saying something like "It's just a date. We're going together to a dinner party for a mutual friend, so we both don't have to go alone." That seems sensible at first, but you have such a good time that one date leads to many more. Suddenly, you fancy yourself in love with the kind of man you said you'd never marry. He has nine kids by his first two marriages and you abhor Rug Rats and besides you said that you would never marry anyone who had failed at more than one marriage. Now what? Control your heartbreaks by controlling your actions in the first place.

If you're not pleased with the way he treats you early in your relationship, dump him immediately. He will only get worse. Everyone—male and female—is on his or her best possible behavior in the early days of a relationship when love colors even the dullest days into beautiful, vivid times. In the beginning, men are normally thoughtful, always call when promised, and bring flowers. As time passes, a relationships inevitably passes into complacency, he unintentionally forgets to call, and months go by between visits from the florists. If the relationship begins with none of the good things, get out quickly. You can rest assured that he won't suddenly decide to start treating you like a princess six months into the relationship.

I am quickly driven to end a budding relationship when a man does not keep his word by phoning at the designated time that he chose or by leaving me "hanging" with partial plans such as "I'll call Sunday afternoon and see what you want to do." Since I've made an agreement to that—and Southern women always keep their word—I refuse other plans and wait out of courtesy for that call. If it doesn't come, I am not a happy little belle. His behavior is not a good sign because it's obvious that the scoundrel is not going to change. I go by the three-strikes rule, so after a stern lecture, he usually gets two more chances and then his phone numbers are erased from my address book. Southern women always make penciled entries for such quick removal.

If you encounter a broken heart that needs to be mended, you may find the same comfort as Southern women by applying the tried-and-true techniques that follow.

Have a good cry. It cleanses the soul and washes poisonous toxins from your body. Do one of two things: Either pick one best friend in the world and cry on her shoulder, or do your crying in the privacy of your own home. Don't let others see you in a vulnerable, pitiful state: mainly because they will remember long after you've forgotten. It's important to maintain your dignity, which encourages your self-esteem to stay healthy and strong. No one likes to be the object of pity, because the image of you as a devastated, destroyed victim will linger in the minds of others long after you have soundly rebounded into another love match.

Immediately pack up all the love letters, photos, and cards. If you want to save them, put them in a box, label it, tape or rubber-band it, and then put it in a remote area of your attic. That way, you won't be tempted to keep reading them. If you don't want to save them, toss them out. One friend keeps all cards and notes in a manila envelope and when the relationship is over, she neatly tosses everything away. It is much easier, she says, than digging through a lot of drawers and closets. Some say that Jill is a cynic, but she claims to be a realist. When all is said and done, most Southern women have a great deal more faith in mankind than that sassy, no-nonsense blonde.

Keep quiet. Don't talk about the breakup incessantly to friends or family. It delays your recovery and bores them.

Remind yourself that it could be worse. Read Gennifer Flowers's autobiographical account of her relationship with Bill Clinton. It'll make you feel much better about your situation.

Throw a brief pity party. Take one night and drown your sorrows in whiskey or ice cream or both. In the South, we prefer straight Jack Daniels because it is distilled in Tennessee

(Southerners are fiercely loyal) and because it is the opposite of anything we would drink normally. Mostly, we're the wine-or-champagne types.

Allow yourself one week to feel sad and lowly. No more. After one week, get over it. Or at least start. Southern women never wallow in misery. We wade through it. Breakups, of course, are easier than death, yet the women of the South face both with courage and firm determination to survive.

My father and the father of my best childhood friend, Lisa, both suffered massive stokes on the same day and died within three days of each other. This gave me the opportunity to closely observe two typically strong Southern women as they dealt with the most devastating blow of their lives. Lisa and I watched in proud admiration as our mothers braved the wretchedly sad heartbreak with grace and positive, inspirational attitudes.

Both women, who had lovingly held their precious husbands in their arms as death mercilessly snatched them from their earthly grasps, never pitied themselves or moaned relentlessly to those around them. They simply talked of the good memories and often repeated how fortunate they had been to have loved such wonderful men for most of their lives. Those many years of happiness, they both agreed, were well worth the pain they now felt over the loss. Southern women are like that—remarkably strong in the face of tragedy and loss.

When your mind drifts to thoughts of him, think of something else. Anything. Memorize your credit card numbers, recite *Beowulf,* or see if you remember all the words to the Lord's Prayer, *America the Beautiful,* or the Gettysburg Address.

Join a health club. Or, if you already have a membership, start going. Focus on self-improvement, which always improves self-esteem. The gym is also a great place to meet guys. One day at my gym, I spotted a new face. I wandered over to another member and remarked, "I didn't know that Maggie was getting a divorce." The woman looked surprised and replied, "I don't think many people know it because it's still kind of a secret. How did you know?" I smiled and answered, "Easy. She joined the gym." Later, I offered my condolences on the failure of another marriage. It was either the fourth or fifth time I had expressed such sentiments to her. "Don't be," she replied airily. "I was looking for a husband—sorry as he was—when I found *him.* I'll find another." And, indeed she did. In about six months.

Focus on his irritating habits. As you work through getting over him, think of those things that drove you up the wall about him. Dwell on those things and not on the good things that you loved. But never discuss those bad things with anyone else.

Oh, be careful what you say. Remember that well-bred Southern women never talk badly about the men we loved emotionally and intimately. Doing so casts a terrible reflection on your judgment because you made such a bad choice. In the South, you can always tell how bad a woman's choice was by how *little* she speaks of him when it's over. If she abruptly changes the subject when asked about him, you know it was *bad.*

Also, the lack of spoken bitterness will give you peace and one day, wanted or not, he'll come back to tell you how much he loved you and what a big mistake he made. Such sweet, sweet words to hear—even ten years down the road.

Don't forget to remember him fondly. Always remember his birthday with a call, note, or card. It's the least you can do for someone who once meant so much to you.

Become self-sufficient. Learn to repair things around your house and mow your own grass. This kind of independence keeps you from feeling desperate to have a man in your life. The bonus is that a lack of desperation also makes it easier to find another man. Desperate women scare off all men—even desperate ones.

Finally, be exceedingly patient with your mother. Promise her that you will only be alone for a short time, that this is merely a detour in your life—not a complete derailing and it isn't the result of any failure on her part. Southern mothers are particularly paranoid about divorced or single daughters, so we get a great deal of practice in soothing nerves and calming anxiety. "No, Mother, you have not failed. It is I who is wretched and selfish by denying you your heart's desire of another son-in-law. I am a lowly creature so completely undeserving of a remarkable woman such as you for my mother." It works perfectly every time. Believe me. I've had enough experience in saying it, so I'm an expert on this little matter.

If your progress tends to be slow, don't fret at all, because some hearts heal slower than other hearts. Just keep reminding yourself that a heart that is broken is better than the breakage of certain other items. After all, it could have been the antique soup tureen from the family china!

And *that* would have been *completely* unbearable.

CHAPTER SEVENTEEN

A GOOD ATTITUDE IS LIKE KUDZU:

IT SPREADS QUICKLY AND NEVER QUITS GROWING

SOUTHERN WOMEN believe in maintaining a good attitude. We preach its virtues as strongly and clearly as a newly ordained minister rails against the wages of sin. We believe, quite simply, that a good attitude is the demarcation line between those who succeed and those who fail in life.

For that reason, Southern women are mindful to extol a bright, optimistic outlook on life: an attitude that is carefully cultivated through good humor, indomitable spirit, formidable optimism, and a steel will (which is a nice way of saying stubbornness). There are those who call our humorous spin on trouble an outrage against the seriousness of life, a totally irreverent way to view the most reverent situations. Yet, we are undeterred. We laugh off those harsh, uninformed criticisms and continue with what we know best—how to survive a challenging life. Yes, we know, as someone once said, that we'll never get out of this life alive. But until then, we intend to live it to the fullest, steadfastly maintaining that everything washes out in the rinse.

We are well aware that attitudes—good, bad, or indifferent—spread as quickly and as strongly as that maliciously clever vine known as kudzu that covers close to a million acres of Southern soil. If you live north of Virginia or farther west of the Mississippi than Louisiana, chances are that you have never seen kudzu vines, which can choke the life, or at least the usefulness, from a plot of ground.

Kudzu may have been created by God, but it was manufactured in Japan and brought to the South in the late 1800s by scientists who proclaimed it to be the perfect solution to the erosion problem that plagued the region. It stopped erosion, but it quickly smothered the land with treacherous green tentacles that attack everything in sight. Nothing is spared.

It grows rapidly and quickly overruns anything in its path—you do not want to leave the children playing anywhere near a kudzu vine because you are apt to come back a couple of hours later, only to hear choked, hoarse cries coming from beneath a massive coverage. If you think that I embellish as Southerners are prone to do, then know that this healthy plant spreads one hundred feet per growing season.

It is sort of a Japanese vegetation version of kamikaze. Except, it refuses to die.

By 1940, five hundred thousand acres across the South were decorated with the large leaves and extraordinarily strong vine of the basically pretty kudzu plant, which climbs utility poles, bridges, and houses. On a farm owned by my family is a building that we suspect was once a farmhouse. It is now a sculptured monument to the formidable strength of kudzu.

My daddy, as a very young man, fought in the South Pacific theater during World War II. I came along when my parents were in their forties, so I can't speak for the years prior to my birth, but I can say that in all the years hence, I never knew my daddy to speak kindly of the Japanese.

My father was dead set against buying Japanese products of any kind, particularly cars. Of course, he did, in fact, buy many Japanese products, but they had American names on them and he never knew the difference. I am only so brazen to impart that piece of information because Daddy has now escaped the toils of this life for that heavenly reward. Otherwise, it would have hastened his departure from this life if he had known that he had unwittingly contributed to the Japanese economy.

It wasn't what he saw in the South Pacific that turned him against the Japanese—or even what happened at Pearl Harbor, for that matter. It was the fact that the Japanese knowingly and willingly sent that maliciously insidious kudzu vine to the States, in general, and to the South, in particular.

"That should have been a warning to us," he remarked solemnly. "We should have known then that those folks were going to be trouble."

I pointed out earlier that Southerners can be great grudge holders; however, Southerners, other than my father's generation, have completely forgiven the Japanese for their part in World War II. But kudzu, now that's another matter.

It is difficult, in fact almost impossible, to destroy kudzu either chemically or by hand. Farmers and landowners try to mow the resilient plant only to have the blades of their bush hogs (that's a big ole tractor) clog up with the strong, stringy vine.

Perhaps by now you can see where I am going with this analogy. Kudzu and Southern women are a lot alike. Both are strong, almost indestructible, lovely, resilient, and refuse to be controlled by men. As further proof of their kinship, the positive attitudes of Southern women spread rapidly and never quit growing.

Just like kudzu.

Plus, they both flourish healthily as a result of the nutrients provided by Southern soil. Once we realized that we were not going to defeat kudzu, we decided to accept it and embrace it as a part of our unique heritage. And, I might point out that we have done quite an admirable job, too.

In Blythewood, South Carolina, there is an annual festival that celebrates the wonderfulness of kudzu. And, yes, there is a Miss Kudzu, who is crowned during the festival, thank you very much. I am told that people come from as far away as Indiana to pay homage to the sacred plant during the Kudzu Festival.

Renowned author James Dickey, who wrote that novel that created an undying stigma for the mountain folks, wrote a poem about it. The Atlanta Zoo named its precious baby gorilla Kudzoo. There is a Kudzu cartoon strip, too.

As you can see, we know how to make the best of a bad situation. We are not a breed of women who will lay down our weary bodies and allow them to be covered by kudzu. We work hard at developing and maintaining good attitudes and positive outlooks, although it is one of the most difficult feats to accomplish. There are certain beliefs and practices that supply Southern women with happy countenances and cheerful dispositions. We believe that:

An attitude is contagious. Whatever it is—good or bad—it spreads. Make your environment as pleasant as possible by having a good, positive attitude. When you are unable to control the negative situations that pellet your life with stress and unhappiness, control your reaction to those situations. Make it positive and optimistic. Wallowing in self-pity and misery will lead you quickly to defeat.

Defeat should never be accepted. In the South, we don't much cotton to the feeling of defeat, which is why we refuse to accept it without a good and just fight. Do what we did with kudzu. If something is not going away and you realize that you're stuck with it for life, peek past the ugliness and see the beauty. It's always there. Sometimes it just takes a little digging.

Setbacks should be viewed as what they are—temporary inconveniences. Sometimes, it takes a setback to reroute our path in life and take us where we wanted to go in the first place—a place we would not have found had we continued on our previous course. When we lose our way and cannot read the directions, an unplanned setback often rights our way. More than a few dreams have come true as a result of temporary inconveniences.

The world can be yours with perseverance and patience. We Southern women are very patient when it comes to getting what we want—even revenge. Keep plugging away, refuse to give up, and one day you will get all that you desire.

Be tenacious in going after what you want. When Southern women go after something they truly want, they're like pit bulldogs clamped down on a piece of raw meat. They refuse to let go. Such tenacity will never fail.

Life should be attacked with gusto. You'll get out of life what you put into it. A sleepy approach produces a sedate, uninteresting life. A vigorous approach that busily juggles home, family, and career will create a fulfilled, happy existence. Busy people are happy people because they don't have time to sit around and fret about the problems of life.

Decisions should be made that will give you peace in the end. So often we say, "Do what you can live with." And, yes, that is important. But it is equally important to make the decisions that will leave you with no regrets on your deathbed. A pleasant end is as important, or perhaps more so, than all the years that came before. In other words, follow your dreams, the ones that fill your heart and give you great hope for the future. Otherwise, you will be filled with tremendous sadness at the end when you realize that you did not take time to do something that was of great importance to you.

Belief in one's self is crucial. You alone are the creator and producer of your life and your dreams. Yes, sometimes life rewrites the script we have perfectly prepared, but roll with the revisions. It doesn't matter how we get to where we want to go. All that matters is that we get there. You have it within your power to do whatever you want and to be whatever you wish. Just switch on the ignition and let it roar.

You should never allow yourself to become embittered. Bitterness is a woman's greatest enemy. It will destroy your ability to live a happy, productive life. Plus it will etch additional horrible, little lines on your lovely face. (Let's not forget to keep our priorities straight, here.) If you can't get over something positively, get even and get it out of your system. But remember that the very best revenge is living well, so take any negative energy and channel it in a positive direction—a direction that will make your life better, which, in turn, will make 'em all pea green with envy. It's our favorite kind of revenge.

Worries and fears should not be verbalized. In the South, we are superstitious and believe that we "can speak things into existence." It may sound like New Orleans voodoo, but actually it turns out to be true too many times. The mind can be a powerful enemy or an ally. It has the ability to defeat us or make us victorious. It's our choice.

So many times in life, when we are struggling or going after something we really want, we tend to think of the times we failed before. Then, before we know it, our minds are filled with defeats that have littered the battlefields of our lives. Stop it before it gets that far. Instead, recall all the successful victories in your life and focus on those. Remember the times when you beat the odds and emerged as a winner. The power of these thoughts will drive you back into Victory Lane.

Of all the words that have gone before, these are the most important because it is a never-give-up attitude that defines Southern women with crystal-clear clarity. We know that attitude either delivers a full life or dictates a slow death as surely as spring resuscitates the roses from a winter's sleep or an early frost prematurely steals the life from those blooms.

An attitude strengthened by toughness, resilience, and constant, hopeful optimism will fiercely and cheerfully overtake the landscape of your life.

Just like kudzu.

About the Author

Ronda Rich is a Southerner who was trained to be courteous, educated to be knowledgeable, and inspired by tradition to be strong and persistent. She has been a sportswriter, a director of corporate communications, and is now a marketing and public relations consultant. She lives in Gainesville, Georgia.

Visit *What Southern Women Know* on the Web at www.southernallure.com (designed and hosted by BellSouth, www.smlbiz.bellsouth.com). Or E-mail Ronda Rich, southswomen@bellsouth.net.